W0090454

30 Minutes
... To Boost Your Self-Esteem

Patricia Cleghorn

Kogan Page

YOURS TO HAVE AND TO HOLD
BUT NOT TO COPY

First published in 1998
Reprinted 2000

Kogan Page Limited
120 Pentonville Road
London N1 9JN

British Library Cataloguing in Publication Data

A CIP record for this book is available from the British Library.

ISBN 0 7494 2667 5

Typeset by BookEns Ltd, Royston, Herts.
Printed and bound in Great Britain by Clays Ltd, St Ives plc

CONTENTS

The 30 Minutes Series

The *Kogan Page 30 Minutes Series* has been devised to give your confidence a boost when faced with tackling a new skill or challenge for the first time.

So the next time you're thrown in at the deep end and want to bring your skills up to scratch or pep up your career prospects, turn to the *30 Minutes Series* for help!

Titles available are:

30 Minutes Before Your Job Interview
30 Minutes Before a Meeting
30 Minutes Before a Presentation
30 Minutes to Boost Your Communication Skills
30 Minutes to Brainstorm Great Ideas
30 Minutes to Deal With Difficult People
30 Minutes to Succeed in Business Writing
30 Minutes to Master the Internet
30 Minutes to Make the Right Decision
30 Minutes to Make the Right Impression
30 Minutes to Plan a Project
30 Minutes to Prepare a Job Application
30 Minutes to Write a Business Plan
30 Minutes to Write a Marketing Plan
30 Minutes to Write a Report
30 Minutes to Write Sales Letters

Available from all good booksellers
For further information on the series, please contact:

Kogan Page, 120 Pentonville Road, London N1 9JN
Tel: 0171 278 0433 Fax: 0171 837 6348

INTRODUCTION

Self-esteem is not a quality bestowed on the lucky few, with everyone else left in the lurch with low self-esteem. Self-confidence can be built. You can learn to boost your own self-esteem. While you may usefully spend a longer time to work out for yourself what makes you feel good, here are some tried and tested approaches which I and my tutors have used over the years with hundreds of people. These will save you time!

It is wonderful if you have a boss who has the time and knowledge to help build the self-esteem of each member of staff. This doesn't happen very often, particularly nowadays when everything is happening so quickly and with increased demands on everyone at work. You may even be the boss, with little idea of how to boost your own self-esteem when the pressure is on, far less anyone else's. You may be one of many thousands in your organization, feeling like a small cog in a large wheel.

With so many people at all levels feeling over-worked and under-valued, it's an *important career skill to be able to boost your own self-esteem. As well as feeling much more confident when you do this, it will motivate you and help you feel back in control of your working life.*

30 Minutes to Boost Your Self-Esteem

It's excellent to want to know how to boost your self-esteem – you have already realized the importance of feeling good about yourself. The key to success and satisfaction not only lies within you but you are the only one that can make the necessary changes in the way you think about yourself. *The power and authority in your life lie with you.* This is regardless of your current circumstances, of whether there is a bad atmosphere at work or one that is making too many demands on you.

Never give up or feel you can't make changes or that you haven't time. Even if you have only a short time to spend, you can boost your self-esteem. You may read the book through or dip into it to choose a way of boosting your self-esteem.

This book is designed to be used when time is short and you're feeling low or when you want that extra edge and sparkle.

8

1

TAKE A MINUTE TO ...

Consider Your True Worth

Self-value

How much do you really value yourself? Do you sometimes feel under-valued and unappreciated? Are there times and situations when you feel lacking in self-worth? Would you like to feel inwardly confident instead of struggling to maintain an outward facade of confidence?

Perhaps more than anything, you want to have a way of giving that confidence to yourself when the pressure is on and you're short of time. So now if you simply let go and take a few minutes, you can start to build a basis of self-esteem that will assist you in moving forward.

Handle self-criticism

You know how unpleasant and how unhelpful it is and how much you dislike it when you're the object of another person's criticism. We're not talking about recommendations at work that will save you time and increase your options, we're talking about carping, insulting remarks, that leave our self-esteem in tatters. Although we may not stand for this from other people, *we often subject ourselves to self-criticism of the very worst kind*. This sort of self-criticism wears you down day after day.

You may feel think 'Oh, it's only words'. *Words are very powerful whether spoken out loud or to yourself.* They have an effect, particularly on you! When other people say something critical about you, you feel angry, put down and yet you can be very capable of putting yourself down. We do this by the thoughts in our heads and by speaking the words out loud to ourselves and others – that is, by going on a self-critical binge.

Appreciate yourself

By the same token you can perk yourself up! That's where your power comes in, your self-esteem, both in letting go of and refusing to continue entertaining these self-critical thoughts and in deliberately looking for things to appreciate about yourself, things that you *are* doing right. Even on a simple level, at the end of each day before you leave your office or place of work, instead of berating yourself for all the things you haven't done or didn't do well, focus on what you have achieved, what you *are* doing well.

How often have you heard people at work say 'I wish they would just show some appreciation', 'I feel like rubbish', 'No-one ever thanks me for the hard graft I put in'? As you may often feel unappreciated in your workplace, you need to be able to give yourself a boost by appreciating yourself. Once you've achieved a task, stop and appreciate how well you are doing, how far you have come, before you go on to the next piece of work and remember to express your appreciation to others.

It is a matter of focus. You are powerful, in charge, because you decide what you want to focus on.

What are three things you have done well or achieved today?

Remember to ask yourself this at the end of each day. Write down your achievements so they can form the basis of your success list!

It's so easy to be critical because it's a habit. Yet you can establish the habit of appreciating yourself instead. Think of the times you've been self-critical today, view these as opportunities to appreciate yourself instead. Notice where you can be more appreciative:

What is one thing you like/appreciate about:
Your body and appearance?
Your attitude to a challenge?
The way you relate to others?
Your contribution at work?

Write down your answers so you can remind yourself of these good points. Each time you find yourself thinking of something you don't like about yourself, also deliberately find something you *do* like. Again write this down, you can look back at these appreciations of yourself next time you're feeling low and add to your appreciation list.

Self-acceptance

While we may want to change and improve ourselves or aspects of our lives, it's still possible and desirable to *appreciate* and accept ourselves as we are *right now*. There will always be aspects that we will want to change and improve. However, you are still worthy of experiencing self-esteem rather than non-acceptance of yourself. In fact, while you won't accept yourself and therefore constantly discourage yourself, your progress is likely to be slow and less pleasant than it could be!

So to boost your self-esteem, set out to make these changes in a spirit of joyful co-operation with yourself. You'll find it easier, quicker and more enjoyable with your own support.

Approve of yourself

Approval – self-approval – is a strong constituent of self-esteem. While at work, for example, you may need to have a proposal approved by your boss or supervisor. This is different from constantly needing the approval of others. Do you often find yourself feeling you have to justify your desires, choices, preferences? Do you provide explanations for these to other people when really it's none of their business? Do you feel disapproved of by others, that they are judgemental of you?

In the course of growing up, a fair amount of disapproval comes our way from the various people in our lives who are 'responsible' for us when we are young. Even though no lasting disapproval is intended, it is easy to see how this happens when we're told 'Oh, you're so lazy', 'don't do that, do this instead', 'you shouldn't', 'you always', 'couldn't you have done better than that?' And so the individual, understandably, feels disapproved of. Not only that, there's a tendency then to feel unworthy and to add your own disapproval of yourself to the chorus, saying to yourself statements like 'I'm so lazy', 'Oh, you fool you should have ...', whether you say these out loud or repeat them to yourself in your head.

An otherwise excellent manager was spending too much time and energy by being overly concerned with whether his boss approved of him. He was able to progress rapidly when he had his own self-approval and gave himself permission to move forward.

Remember, the person whose approval you so badly want may be wanting *your approval!* Constantly comparing yourself to others, wasting energy on that, will create self-disapproval rather than self-approval. The antidote to all this disapproval is lots of approval! So *really start now to step up your level of self-approval*.

- What is one situation where it would help you to have more self-approval?
- Who do you feel you need more self-approval with?
- Is there a work-related situation where it would help you to have more self-approval?
- What about at home with your family or friends?
- Are there other times, perhaps socially, when more self-approval will help you?

Identify these times, writing them down so you can refer to them to bring in more approval of yourself, for example before being with a particular person and while you are with them. Do the same with the other situations that you have considered.

Give yourself permission to move forward

Giving yourself permission is also part of self-approval. Notice if there are things you are holding back on. This may be in relation to what you would love to do because they would be enjoyable. Perhaps you are pressuring yourself to work instead or you may feel you haven't quite enough self-approval to start something new. Could you allow yourself to move forward with your own self-approval rather than waiting for that approval from anyone else? After our programmes people report that when they boost their level of self-esteem, their self-approval helps them to take on new opportunities and situations. Are there aspects of your life you are now willing to move forward?

Self-esteem boosters

- Stop self-criticism. Next time you go on a self-critical binge, don't allow yourself to continue – halt the flow of critical thoughts and even think of something you appreciate about yourself instead.
- Notice your good points and what you *are* achieving. Write them down and keep them as reminders to yourself.
- Practise accepting yourself, especially when you're feeling judgemental.
- Bring in self-approval as often as you can today, check your self-approval 'quotient' throughout the day.
- Give yourself permission to move forward in one way this week. What steps will you now take?

Keynote booster

Keynote boosters can be used for a day or more, then use another booster of your choice.

Take a minute ... several times today to practise the three As of self-esteem:

Appreciate yourself, **A**ccept yourself and **A**pprove of yourself.

2

ATTITUDE IS ALL

Do You Have The Right Attitude *To Yourself*?

Your thoughts – do they help or hinder you?

The person it is most important to have the right thoughts and attitude to is *you*. Take a moment to consider. Are your thoughts about yourself helpful? That is, do they support all you want to have, become and do? There is little point in having a goal to achieve something, whether that's gaining promotion at work or completing a qualification that will help you in your career, if you constantly tell yourself 'I'll never be able to do this' or 'I'm not good enough'.

At best, you'll make the process more difficult and more unpleasant than it need be, and at worst you'll put yourself off altogether by your low self-esteem thoughts. These thoughts can also be picked up by others, however much of an outer show of confidence and bravado you put on. And conversely when you do feel you're good enough, when you do feel good about yourself, you will still want to take the appropriate steps, yet you won't need to try so hard to impress: people will *know*.

Self-esteem thoughts for results

People at work frequently set goals and project targets. While they may deal with any logistical and strategic objections, the *thoughts* of those on their team are rarely taken into consideration. It is highly practical for everyone in a team to be aware of the power of their thoughts. With regard to your individual contribution, while taking all the practical steps you need, notice if you are telling yourself low self-esteem thoughts like 'I'm not good enough', 'I can't do this well', 'other people are doing better'. You'll slow yourself down and make the process more difficult and less enjoyable. Change these thoughts so that you remind yourself that you are good enough, you are doing well enough, also that your contribution is of value, regardless of whether this is fully appreciated.

We've seen that the most common 'downers' to your self-esteem are indulging in a self-critical 'binge', letting unhelpful thoughts go unchecked so you end up constricting your vision of yourself and the world. You remedy this by each time these 'downers' pervade your mind, you say 'stop' and make a concerted effort to choose thoughts that are helpful – 'I am good enough', 'I can handle this', 'I deserve to have this work out'.

You can choose what you want to think

So your thoughts can actually help or hinder you. Low-level, unhelpful thoughts like 'I'm not good enough', 'I can't do this', 'it's because it's me', 'someone else could do better', 'I'm not quick/intelligent/organized enough', 'I'm too …', all these are low-level self-esteem thoughts which, when you are unguarded and repeat them often enough, will begin to make you feel like a failure. The important thing is to remember that *you always have a choice of what you want to think*.

It can be quite a revelation when you realize that your thoughts are not random things that happen to you, but that you can control your mind! You need to *want* to do this, to realize that with determination you can choose thoughts that are helpful to you. So when you realize that you're subjecting yourself to a torrent of unhelpful thinking, you can choose to stop and boost your self-esteem instead by having supportive thoughts.

With regard to relationships, if you consistently have unhelpful critical thoughts, particularly if you say them out loud about the other person, your relationship will tend to go downhill. Conversely, if you focus on what is *right* with the person, their kindness to you, for example, then that will help your relationship. *What you put your attention on tends to increase*. Your thinking can make a relationship or situation worse or better.

Choose helpful thoughts

To boost your self-esteem, let go of any unhelpful thoughts as soon as you realize you're thinking of them. Make up a more helpful thought instead. So instead of saying 'I'll never be able to do this' say 'I'm making progress with this step by step'. Instead of saying 'Oh, I'm not good enough' say '*I am good enough*'.

Fashion your thoughts to help you as an individual so that they are in line with who you are and what you want to achieve. This also contributes considerably to any group or team effort because everyone is then giving of their best in a way that is best for them. *Choosing helpful thoughts affects your whole feeling of confidence, well-being and motivation.*

Self-esteem boosters

- Emphasize *helpful* thoughts and let go of unhelpful ones, reminding yourself of the helpful ones throughout each day.
- Just see unhelpful thoughts disappearing, imagine them in your mind's eye, rub them off a board with a magic cleaner or picture them fading and disappearing.
- Take a minute when you're feeling low to write out your unhelpful thoughts, put a line through them and change them to helpful ones so that 'I'm not good enough' becomes 'I am good enough', 'I can't do this' becomes 'I can do this'.
- Turn down the volume on thoughts that don't help. Imagine helpful thoughts being repeated in a voice you find appealing.
- What would a person who wants to feel good and have certain results need to be thinking? For example, 'I'm doing very well', 'I'm successful'. Add your own thoughts.

Keynote booster

Keynote boosters can be used for a day or more, then use another booster of your choice.

Take a minute ... several times today to use the thought 'I'm good enough to ...', completing it in different ways.

3

EMOTIONS

Surely Not At Work!

Managing your emotions

Learning how to manage, that is, to integrate your emotions, is one of the most important practical lessons we can learn with regard to boosting self-esteem. Many conflicts, unspoken as well as spoken, are difficult to handle because of low self-esteem. Nothing prompts us to feel worse and to be less productive at work than feeling trapped by our own emotions. Self-doubt and defensiveness lead to fault finding, resentment, and, in business terms, low productivity. Not the best recipe for business success! If you don't feel good about yourself, your service to others isn't going to be very good either.

When you do not come from a point of self-esteem, you can find yourself embroiled in all sorts of upsets which are wasteful of your time and destructive of your energy. They can actually make you feel ill or certainly exhausted. You're likely to have experienced this with the increased pace and pressure of work nowadays. More emotions of anger and helplessness are provoked and a desperate attempt is made either to control them, often by denying them, or expressing them in an outburst.

Emotions suppressed at work are more dangerous because they're more likely to erupt. When very strenuously denied under the cover of being 'neutral' they often explode at the wrong time!

Accept *all* your feelings

Upset feelings of one member of staff or between people at work waste more time and resources than anything else. Rather than bottling up your feelings, be aware within *yourself* which emotions you're experiencing. Be aware of the discomfort you are experiencing. For example, that uncomfortable feeling in your stomach is not what you had for lunch but was caused by your reaction to what the person who you were having lunch with was saying! As far as you can, always acknowledge to yourself what you're feeling – for example, isolated, angry, sad, frustrated. Then you can decide if it's appropriate to communicate your feelings. Sometimes it is and sometimes it's not.

What *is* important is that you relax, let yourself feel your feelings, communicate, if appropriate, and take steps that you feel are important to put in place.

Remember that you cannot dictate how other people behave. While you cannot accept bad behaviour, what will help you most is to be in charge of your own emotions, to be able to feel them and let them go. The more you pretend to yourself that you're not feeling anything or that you are 'neutral', the longer these emotions will linger and the more exhausted and distracted you will feel as you suppress them. *To boost your self-esteem, accept your feelings rather than denying or suppressing them or expressing them inappropriately.*

When someone presses your buttons!

With anger and fear, when what you feel is out of proportion to the situation, three things may be occurring:

1. You may be reacting to past pain that you've not yet resolved.
2. You may be out of harmony with yourself and your life, that is, feeling bad about yourself.
3. You may feel others have not been treating you the way you feel you should be treated.

You can resolve this by gently feeling your emotions and letting them go. Get in balance by using your self-esteem booster thoughts and actions. You can change your beliefs about yourself, other people and situations. Don't put up with unkind behaviour. Treat yourself well. Notice that when others aren't able to do this, it's a reflection on them, not on you. Whatever you decide to communicate or to do, it's very important now to refocus on yourself and what is important to you.

Resentment at work or in any other area of life causes problems. Little practical work is achieved when you focus all your energy on a problem, on how much you dislike a person or the way they are behaving. Then you feel bad and find it difficult to focus on what *is* important. It can be difficult to communicate without resentment so tackling the underlying causes and feelings within yourself are important if you're to move ahead clearly.

When we feel another person is deliberately being unkind and unfair to us, it is difficult to handle. Your upset feelings affect your self-esteem and your ability to function in all areas of your life. Even when we get the person to stop or change their offending behaviour, unless we change our minds about it and raise our self-esteem, we'll still have to deal with our feelings when the next person comes along and 'does this to us' so that we feel affected in a similar way.

Letting go of hurt feelings

A big 'downer' to our self-esteem is when we short-circuit ourselves by either bottling things up and denying our feelings or saying something hurtful to the other person. Neither of these work. Before you read on, don't beat yourself up if you recognize that's what you tend to do. We do this when we allow our mind and emotions to get caught up with fears and worry over the past and the future. With repetitive negative thoughts, it is almost as though the needle is stuck on the record of an old gramophone.

Recognize when you start to do this because it can be a vicious circle. You do it when you're feeling low and stressed and that makes you feel even lower. So stop, relax, start changing your mind and raising your self-esteem. Let go. Then deliberatetly change your mind, focus on helpful thoughts and on what is important to you.

When you feel you're stressing yourself inordinately and your self-esteem is in tatters, you need to deal with the upset you're experiencing in a way that will boost your self-esteem and not make you feel worse about yourself:

1. Acknowledge to yourself your hurt feelings and see it not as a plot to hurt you but as coming from the other person's ignorance, lack of respect.
2. Let go of blaming them. To help yourself feel better and move on, each time you find yourself dwelling on the person and their behaviour, let go and focus on something better and brighter in your own life.
3. Change your own thoughts to 'I am doing well', 'I am supported', whatever thoughts you need to help you.

4. Do for yourself whatever makes you feel good, comfortable, relaxed and also move your attention from the distraction and focus on what is important to *you*.

With self-esteem you can learn to let go of hurt feelings yet communicate clearly to focus on and ask for what you want. Emotions just are, they're not right or wrong. Listen to them – they can put you in touch with what you want. Learning to give yourself what you want can dissolve your anger and any harshness towards yourself and others.

Lighten up your feelings

You can learn to bring in happy, lighter emotions when you choose. With higher self-esteem we really can be much happier more of the time. We may be used to feeling low so changing the habit requires practice. You know what it feels like when you feel good about yourself, with things that are important to you working out. Good feelings can be prompted by a visit from a friend, completing a project successfully at work, spending even a short time doing something you enjoy, or a kiss from your child. Now imagine those good feelings. Remember them. Let yourself experience them again. As part of self-esteem you can experience more happiness, joy and peace by choosing these feelings for yourself.

Self-esteem boosters

- Ask yourself daily at different times not so much 'What do I think?' but 'What am I *feeling*?' 'How do I *feel* about this?'
- Relax and feel your feelings, don't block them, they'll flow and go.

- When you are really angry, do something physical, for example 'chop a log of wood' or walk round the block. This will help to integrate emotions at least short term.
- To stop upsetting patterns repeating, let go of resentment. Ideally acknowledge your feelings then let go of blaming.
- Learn to communicate your feelings without blaming. This takes practice but it's well worth it.
- Refocus on yourself and what is important to you and gives you joy.
- Learn to bring in good feelings, remember times when you have been happy, at peace, joyful. Remember and then focus on those feelings so you can bring in the experience of them now.

Keynote booster

Keynote boosters can be used for a day or more, then use another booster of your choice.

Take a minute ... several times today to make friends with your feelings. Enjoy your emotions or let them go.

HARMONY, SWEET HARMONY!

Self-Esteem For Improved Relationships At Work

Harmony begins with you. To keep your self-esteem high, and this is really the only way you can perform at an optimum level, pay attention to your interactions with others. Even when no harsh words are spoken, you can have much resentment and anger between people. So for self-esteem, 'correct' this at source by integrating your feelings, that is, acknowledging how you feel to yourself and then letting the feelings move and change.

When there is bitchiness or bullying from either sex, don't let it get you down. It's important to bring what is happening to your colleagues' attention and again this may require self-esteem. Take things as far as you can, then refocus on yourself and what is important to you rather than letting this behaviour be totally distracting to you.

In an emergency, take a deep breath, count to 10, anything that helps you stabilize and get centred. Revenge seldom works and good relationships with a colleague or a customer are required long term for a harmonious outcome that lasts. Make time to reflect, to decide what your objectives are long term. Work on your self-esteem to help you achieve this desired outcome rather than wasting your time on who is right and who is wrong.

Self-esteem for everyone

You can very often get low group self-esteem. There's no need to be affected and in fact you can raise the level of the group's self-esteem by refusing to be sucked in. Remember, *you choose*. It's so common to find everyone in a group or department or even a company moaning and groaning about how bad things are. This also lowers everyone's self-esteem, their motivation and morale.

Everyone likes to feel appreciated for their contribution and it has a wonderful effect on self-esteem. Yet appreciation is rarely expressed. Even a little will go a long way and can be so helpful in boosting morale. Even if you're not the boss, try it with your colleagues and see how much better people feel about themselves.

Another aspect of self-esteem and relating to others is when you compare yourself with others, leading to internal rivalries at work. There may be jealousy, feeling someone's getting something that you deserve. So make sure that you are noticed by all means, be high-profile, yet also build your self-esteem and let go of resentment, focusing on yourself and your abilities rather than wasting any time in putting another person down.

Sometimes you may feel low self-esteem because you feel another person, maybe someone close to you at work, is not paying enough attention to you or putting their appreciation in the direction of someone else. You may want to be sure you have their loyalty. While it's appropriate to expect to come first with a spouse, at work you may get attention and support yet you cannot expect to have emotional support all the time.

Who is responsible for how *you* feel?

In truth, only you can be emotionally responsible for yourself. No other person can do it for you nor is it appropriate for you to be the emotional caretaker of any other person. You can't be responsible for how they're feeling all the time, nor can you make them happy. Whether it's your boss or a colleague, to attempt to do this will drain your energy and affect your self-esteem, especially if they seem unwilling to do much to help themselves. You will want to be kind to other people, yet you cannot ensure or be responsible for their state of mind. Each individual needs to do that for himself or herself. It will lower your self-esteem and energy if you're constantly trying to do this for another individual.

From your own point of view, it's better if you're able to do this for yourself, that is, be able to boost your own self-esteem. Then you can clearly ask for what you want rather than demanding it and needing it to keep your self-esteem high. This is the difference between loving to have approval, appreciation, support or asking for it on a professional basis and, on the other hand, being desperate, which is never an attractive proposition!

Self-respect and respect for others

For improved relationships, what you're aiming at is to treat everyone well and with respect, including yourself. This is not in any way to suggest that you are falsely nice yet unfair to yourself. The clearer you are about what's appropriate for you, the more clearly you can ask for what you want and the easier you will find it to give a high level of attention to colleagues and customers.

Self-esteem boosters

- Remember to express appreciation daily to colleagues, especially of a job well done.
- Let go of resentment when you notice it creeping in.
- What can *you* do to help a situation at work, where there is a challenge, perhaps misunderstandings?
- To promote harmony and co-operation, set mutual goals with high self-esteem thoughts.

Keynote booster

Keynote boosters can be used for a day or more, then use another booster of your choice.

Take a minute ... several times today to focus on the word *harmony* and what that means to you at work. What is one step you can take to create greater harmony at work?

5

JUST A WORD ...
ABOUT CRITICISM

Bring Self-Esteem Into The Picture

Criticism without taking self-esteem into account can be unhelpful, both for the giver and the receiver. When your work is being criticized, particularly when appreciation has not been forthcoming, it can be difficult to feel valued for your overall contribution. Let yourself feel your feelings, let go of them, integrate them. That is, relax, feel them, they'll change. It is helpful to do this at home or at least on your own. You may also want to let off steam by confiding in a trusted friend or partner outside the work environment.

Then look objectively at what is being said, stall for time rather than reacting right away. Be willing to do what's appropriate if what is suggested is an improvement and not making unreasonable demands on you.

The importance of self-esteem

When your self-esteem is high you are less likely to feel demoralized and you'll also be able to make your case more clearly. So many of these issues are about personalities, power play, not about deciding objectives and meeting them. If you have a boss or a colleague with a problem, you may experience daily carping as a result of *their* low self-esteem. It's especially difficult with those who, through low self-esteem, drive themselves without respect and do the same to others! So keep your self-esteem high and look for ways in which you can improve your situation. Get support to improve things, both within the company and perhaps by looking outside it.

Communicate clearly and with compassion

When you want to put your point across, some reflection will help you identify what it is appropriate for you to say so you can do so more clearly and with respect for yourself and the other person or people.

When you want to communicate your feelings about another's actions or lack of them, be specific: 'when you ... I feel ...' or if you don't want to reveal your feelings, 'when you do x, y happens ...'. For example, you might say either:

'I feel hurt when you don't support me at meetings' or 'When you don't support me at meetings we look like a weak team'.

You can ask for what you'd like to happen or the other person to do and say why. You can use persuasion by tying in what you see as the results of their compliance or the reverse. Try to avoid making it too much like a threat or a promise! For example:

'I'd like us to support each other then we can gain more backing from other Sections.'

Self-esteem needs to come into the picture with all communications at work. It is not being too aggressive or passive and, above all, it is being appropriate to the situation. Notice if you often put down yourself and others. Whether you feel your comments are justified or not, that is always going to bring your own energy down.

As well as taking appropriate action, reframe what you want to say in a more positive way and that will immediately help. From a point of self-esteem, don't get off-balance, off-centre, by matching energy if you have to deal with an angry person. Communicate clearly and with compassion.

Goodwill

From a self-esteem angle, always look at what is the intention behind your communication. It would be very different if it was to put down a person, make them wrong or to come up with a harmonious solution. If you're in the position of seeing another person every day or regularly at work, you will need to aim for a harmonious relationship with them. This does not mean you need to have lunch with them once a week or drinks after work, yet do all you can to seek to dissolve the animosity. Do this by working on your self-esteem and dissolving it within yourself first. With goodwill, all communications, even 'criticisms', go better.

The quality of your relationship with the person or other people involved will always be there as an important factor. For self-esteem, we can decide that we will communicate in a way that promotes ongoing harmonious relationships, trust and co-operation.

Self-esteem boosters

- What specifically makes you feel a particular way or results in certain circumstances? Be specific: 'when you do ... I feel ...' not 'Oh, you always do ...'.
- What do you want? What would you prefer the other person to do? Again, don't expect others to read your mind.
- What benefits would come from a change in behaviour, actions, attitude or what would be a disadvantage in not making this change?
- Can you express what you want to say more clearly and more compassionately?
- What other steps can you take to move forward, refocusing on yourself?

Notice there will be many times that our communication doesn't meet the ideal, so relax, let yourself off the hook.

Keynote booster

Keynote boosters can be used for a day or more, then use another booster of your choice.

Take a minute ... several times today to check the *clarity* and *compassion* of all your communications – ask 'Is this true?' and 'Is this helpful?'

6

SPOTLIGHT ON YOU!

Self-Esteem For Interviews, Meetings, Pay-Rise Requests And Presentations

Does a lack of self-esteem let you down at interviews and meetings? Do you back out of giving presentations? Are you too scared to ask for a pay-rise? In any situation where you feel you are being 'judged' by others, it is important to be able to raise the level of your self-esteem.

It's also important to attend to external factors and I would refer you to some of the excellent books in this series for that. However, it's equally important to prepare yourself on an *inner* level. So to make sure you are confident, the most important thing to bring in is *self-approval*. You can learn to, not boast, but maintain a steady confidence that sits lightly on you, as this is what will be picked up from you by others.

Your inner image

Your *inner image* is all you think and feel about yourself.

Raising your self-esteem will help you to feel better about any challenging situation. Also when you're feeling less than confident about yourself, this is going to be picked up by others, however glossy your exterior may be. And anyway, why suffer within yourself when boosting your self-esteem can assist you in getting through the situation graciously, perhaps even enjoyably?

Meetings

Preparation as to the purpose and content of the meeting is going to be very helpful to you. Yet preparation on an inner level is also very practical, to give you the confidence to show what you know. There's nothing more infuriating, as you may already have experienced, than not having the confidence to speak up with what you know or your ideas and then have someone else put them forward. So as well as knowing what you want to say and how it fits into the scheme of things, it's having the confidence to do this.

Bring in self-approval. Work daily on your self-esteem, not just right before the meeting. Practise, out loud to yourself, how you will make your main points and counter any criticisms calmly and with confidence.

While your role will determine your behaviour to a certain extent – whether you're head of a company, a manager, chairing the meeting, or you have just started at a junior level – what you have to say is important and deserves to be heard.

Appraisals

Appreciation is often forgotten! Appreciation of a person's good points is played down by some organizations, which isn't encouraging. If you're 'receiving' an appraisal, prepare for the meeting. Don't over-react, nor of course accept put-downs or sign statements that are unfounded. Whether you're the giver or receiver, remember to respect yourself and the other person, then it's easier to agree and act on recommendations without ill-feeling.

Asking for a pay-rise

Depending on what was said at your appraisal, this may be the right time to ask about a pay-rise. Certainly do it well before salary reviews. Do some research. Know the wage structure, and the way employees are ranked. Make sure you approach the right person when you ask for more money – responsibility might be with either personnel or management, so get the right one.

Then prepare yourself. It's very important to build up a sense of self-value. You have to have outward evidence that you are an achiever, but on a more subtle level you need self-esteem – you need to have an *'inner CV'* of the good qualities and abilities you have. There mustn't be a flicker of doubt in your mind, or it will be like trying to sell something when you have a sneaking suspicion about its value. So check how you think of yourself – if you are beset by self-doubt, just gently change your thoughts around. Negative thoughts can impede your progress and even stop you asking for your rise, so convert them into helpful ones. It's also really helpful if you can learn to integrate your emotions – recognize what you're feeling, let them move and change. Don't bottle up feelings like fear of asking for more money, anger at not being offered it, or even desperation. If you do, they may well be present in the actual conversation you have with the relevant person and experienced by them as 'negativity'.

If you are told 'no', find out if it's simply because you've asked at the wrong time. Ask to talk further. Try to avoid closing on a 'no'. You may need to persist – subtly, so they don't disappear when they see you approaching.

It's also important to consider that if you're doing a lot and not getting recognition your next pay-rise may be with another company!

Presentations

Have the self-esteem to *prepare*, whether you have two months or two minutes. Focus on the content and the ways of putting your message across that are appropriate to your audience. However, you also need to prepare by building self-esteem, so you have the confidence to be flexible should that be required and the confidence to deal with questions, challenges even. If you can do this without a hint of controlled anger or becoming defensive or aggressive, that will help you. Any edge is likely to be picked up by your audience.

Remember, however immaculate your appearance and argument, people want someone they can trust, someone who has confidence in themselves!

Practise your self-esteem. How as a person with self-esteem will you speak, walk in, conduct yourself in this important situation? See this in your mind's eye as you relax and imagine the scene.

Interviews

There will be outer preparation of your application, CV, research on the company and the position for which you are applying. Yet your *'inner CV'* is equally important – your thoughts and feelings about yourself, your own estimation of yourself. You can't expect other people to be fully accepting and approving of you if you don't feel that way about yourself! So work on those self-esteem boosters!

As part of your preparation for interviews, bring in your recognition of your good qualities and abilities. Have an appreciation of what you have to offer that is special. What will you bring that is unique to this job? Make a list that you can refer to and add to, then relax. Trust that if you do your preparation and give a confident response, and if this is the right job for you, you will get it.

If you're going for an interview after having been made redundant, it's especially important to remember that you're still of great value, regardless of your current status. So don't judge yourself as not being of value. Work then on building your self-esteem, know your market value but also know and be able to demonstrate your worth and value. Feel sure of that within yourself.

Going for and getting interviews for jobs you don't want for the 'experience' won't necessarily boost your self-esteem and may waste a considerable amount of your time. For an interview, although you can prepare questions you think you will be asked, when things go differently you may feel thrown. So when you're not asked what you expected or feel it's going badly, thinking, 'I've blown it', don't despair and let your self-esteem shrink. Instead, relax, bring your self-approval back so you can centre yourself. Muster your resources to get back in the flow of the interview and do yourself credit!

Self-esteem boosters

- Practise bringing in self-approval so you can experience that at will.
- Practise relaxing when you feel nervous so that this becomes your new response.
- Once again remind yourself of your good qualities, abilities and times when you've been successful.

- Practise some of what you'll say and repeat those things with confidence.
- Bring in self-esteem thoughts to boost your self-esteem, both before your interview, meeting or presentation, and during it.

Keynote booster

Keynote boosters can be used for a day or more, then use another booster of your choice.

Take a minute ... several times today as you prepare for an important event to do your *inner preparation* – that is, boost your self-esteem.

7

BUFFER STRESS WITH SELF-ESTEEM

Boosting Your Self-Esteem Helps Control Stress

Low self-esteem as a stressor

Research shows that low self-esteem is the biggest cause of stress. Low self-esteem thoughts bring your energy down – thoughts like, 'I knew this would happen', 'I'll never be able to', 'I can't', 'I'm nowhere near good enough', 'other people manage better'. When we feel bad about ourselves and under pressure, it makes it more difficult to perform at work or to move forward. The first step is to get those self-esteem thoughts in place. That will lift your energy and make it easier to centre yourself to do what needs to be done.

The best use of your time

With regard to controlling stress, look at what you can

achieve and actually do. Take a moment to reflect from a point of self-esteem, that is, to listen to yourself with regard to the best use of your time and energy. This will save you time and energy, perhaps a considerable amount of it. You can see more clearly what you need to do and you may also have some more understanding of your situation. Remember, in times of stress, to be extra gentle rather than harsh towards yourself and others, both in how you think and speak and how you treat yourself and them.

Of course pressures can come from all directions at the same time. There are times when many people have high expectations. It can be difficult to stay focused and complete what needs to be done, even when you want to. Feeling that you're wasting your time, trying to accomplish too many things is a sure way to create stress. You can reverse this by working on your self-esteem. Learn to relax. Identify what is important, both in what you need to achieve and the steps you need to take to do so. Then you can prioritize activities whether you will be doing them or by delegating them.

Keep your energy level high

You can look after your energy by keeping the level of your self-esteem high. Part of this will be listening to and monitoring what is important to you as you go about your business. When you feel better about yourself, you're also more likely to play your full part in the proceedings or project.

If *you* don't look after yourself, for example by preventing yourself getting over-strained and over-tired, no one else is going to! The quality of your contribution and your ability to sustain this will be helped by your looking after yourself – that is self-esteem in practice. Self-care is good for business and particularly noticeable when customer service is vital to your work. *You can give an extra-special service and quality of attention to others only when you know how to maintain your self-esteem on a daily basis.*

When you start to drive yourself, check if it's important to to be engaged in those activities. If it is, then perhaps take more frequent rests if you are tired, stopping earlier to do something completely different. You will be able to complete work of a higher quality in a shorter time if you do this and look after your energy.

You are unique

Low self-esteem and stress can come from ignoring both your intuition, that is, your hunches about what to do and what is best for you, and your individuality. The two are linked. Only you can determine what is appropriate for you as an individual – you are unique. If you are trying to build your life on someone else's 'shoulds', you will experience stress and frustration.

Start to get to know yourself by listening to your own intuition and desires. You know best what *is* right for you.

Practical relaxation

Taking time to learn to relax your body totally is another excellent way to control stress. You need to be on your own, sitting or lying down comfortably. Put on some relaxing music if you like or else have total peace and quiet. Then gently relax your body, your head to your toes, tensing each part and then relaxing it if that is better for you. Keep your breathing relaxed. Let go of any busy thoughts and pull your attention back to you. Focus on pleasant, helpful thoughts and good feelings. Picture pleasant outcomes to various situations. Take 10–20 minutes on this. Then take a moment before gently opening your eyes. Wait another minute before gently getting up.

As you get used to what it feels like to be relaxed, you will become more aware of when you're *starting* to get stressed. You will find it easier to immediately bring in a feeling of relaxation.

Letting go of fear

Fear is a great sapper of self-esteem and a stressor. Self-doubt and fear leave little room for self-esteem. You're also likely to use your time and energy, not in ways that help the situation but which pull down your self-esteem. When your self-esteem needs a boost because you're feeling fear over the future or remorse over the past, let go of any fear you have been feeling. Determine that you will use your energy to take a leap forward from negativity to helping yourself even more. Relax as you do this, so that you come from determination not desperation.

Other people as stressors!

When you're experiencing fear and low self-esteem thoughts, you will be at your most stressed. If part of what is tiring you is being with people you find draining, then keep relaxing when you're with them yet don't allow your time with them to continue any longer than is necessary. You may also feel extra sensitive to other people's demands, opinions and criticisms. While doing what you need to with regard to your work and personal responsibilities, you need to draw back, at least in your mind, from people who seem unsupportive or 'too much' right now.

Bring balance into your life – make time for *you*

If you've become low through a period of over-work or with worrying about changes, job security and prospects, then while continuing to acknowledge the importance of this, practise daily relaxation. Remembering to be extra gentle with yourself, schedule in at least one thing you enjoy each day, even 15 minutes of time for *you* works wonders.

People report that giving that 15 minutes to something they enjoy is a great self-esteem booster. To reduce stress and boost your self-esteem, don't delay in giving time also to personal relationships, even if you're very busy. Then you can create more *balance in your life*, more of what you want. You'll be boosting your self-esteem and as you boost your self-esteem, you get in an upward cycle, spiralling upwards. You can then give to yourself and those who are important to you more of what makes you flourish!

Self-esteem boosters

- Be persistent in changing unhelpful thought patterns and in reinforcing a helpful way of thinking. Learn to recognize your emotions. Accept and experience them so they cause less stress and exhaustion.
- Take a minute to stop and check that you're treating yourself and others with respect when you and they may be feeling fraught.
- Learn the steps to practical relaxation and do some daily.
- Check your life-style is in balance; it's important to make time for friends, family and creative interests. Take a moment to put 'dates' in your diary and keep to them.
- Do not be afraid to ask for support from family and friends or advice from professionals. Make a note of those who can help you and arrange to see them

informally or by making an appointment. Your first step is that telephone call!

■ Look for something extra, however small, you really enjoy doing each day. Remember to treat yourself gently.

Keynote booster

Keynote boosters can be used for a day or more, then use another booster of your choice.

Take a minute ... several times today to have any stress remind you to relax your body totally, let go and say to yourself 'all *is* well'.

8

WORK CHOICES AND CHANGES

The Right Work For *You* Is A Must For Self-Esteem

Shape your future

We spend so much time at work that you owe it to yourself from a point of self-esteem, if your work isn't currently satisfying, to find out if there is work that would be more suited to you, that you could enjoy and where you can make your best contribution. If you consistently feel you're wasting your time in the job you're in, maybe you are! Ongoing low self-esteem is linked with dissatisfaction at work. Have the courage to find out what would be satisfying and joyful for you and move towards that.

With the rapid pace of change at work you may not feel in charge of decisions made about your job. With self-esteem, however, you can be in charge of the way you act and react. You are in charge of *shaping the future for yourself*.

A heart-search for a job-search!

Having the intention to and actively looking for the right job for you may mean looking within yourself as well as at the job market, that is, a heart-search as well as a job-search. If you do this while still in your current job, you may experience less of the uncertainty of not having a job. It is an opportunity to have the project of finding the right job for you, in your own time, that is for *you* as an individual with your unique qualities and requirements. It's worth spending time on this.

The self-esteem to go for it!

While in your current job, you also need to raise the level of your energy and your self-esteem. Then you can use that self-esteem to act as a springboard for moving forward into the right work for you.

When you feel you are in 'the wrong job', it is difficult to provide more than, at best, an 'adequate' service for others. The best work is done by those in a job that's right for them and this is particularly noticeable in the service industries. You may have experienced a time in your working life when your job felt like a drag, when it was all you could do to get yourself to work and through your workload, never mind quality attention to yourself, colleagues or customers!

Remember your value and worth

Very often our self-esteem is low when we realize that the nature of the work we're doing will not change and it's not something we now enjoy. Sometimes work that was appropriate for us at one time may no longer be so, say, five years later. Being in the wrong job relentlessly with no sign of change will have an effect on your self-esteem. Being without a job, especially for a long period of time, will also affect your self-esteem. Regardless of your current job status, even if you're in a job you don't like, even if you've been made redundant or are a young person who's finding difficulty getting the right job, *you are of great value and your contribution is important.* It's essential to remind yourself of this daily.

If you consistently stay in a job you don't like, without the motivation of a sense of achieving more, that is, of larger purpose, your self-esteem and well-being will continue to suffer.

Making the best of a bad job

While it's not usually appropriate to change jobs suddenly or to leave a job you don't like, while you look for something better, it's well worth thinking if there's a way of making your current job better before you go for a major change. That in itself will boost your self-esteem.

Notice the benefits of your current job, especially if you feel you have to look very hard for them! Even if it's one of those jobs where nothing is as good as leaving it. It will help your self-esteem to feel that you've made the best job that you could.

Could you make more of a contribution or are you putting in too much work and needing to, for example, leave work earlier to get on with things you love to do? This may be a hobby, time for yourself, enjoying yourself with family and friends.

It may be that other things like making small changes to your work area, taking a lunch break with food you enjoy, wearing clothes you look good in to work, help to tide you over. Sometimes doing what you can to create harmony with another person you've been having difficulty with can make things bearable.

Rather than feeling it doesn't matter because you know you're leaving anyway, boost your self-esteem to aim for this harmony. *Then you can carry goodwill with you to the next job.*

Redundancy

Sometimes you may be in the position of having to make a job change because you have been made redundant. Not much of a choice! You may well experience strong feelings about the way you've been treated. It's easy then to undervalue yourself. Bring in a sense of self-esteem. Remember you *are* of value, you have all your special qualities and abilities regardless of your job status. Remind yourself that you can get a job that is right for you and let go of upset feelings. Be determined and focus on finding work that is appropriate for you. Treat yourself gently and build up your energy to persevere with your job-search. Have faith in yourself and your ability to succeed. Be open to opportunities!

The right job for you

While in your current job, have as a personal project the aim of finding work you enjoy. You may know what you want. If not, by all means take psychometric tests, careers counselling, read books on different types of work and visit different organizations you feel would be appropriate. Yet, be aware that the main indicator is a self-esteem one, that is, when you do or even imagine yourself doing this activity, this type of work, do you feel better about yourself, do you feel a sense of energy, purpose, a sense of joy?

Start from what you enjoy. You can tell when you feel more enthusiastic, lighter, more joyful, that you are moving in the right direction.

Sometimes an activity you regard as a hobby will take an

important place in your life. You will realize that you want to spend more and more time on it. Perhaps it's something you make or a service you could receive payment for. As you boost your self-esteem, you will realize that in due course you will be set to make money from doing work you enjoy.

The bigger picture

You need to look at the bigger picture. Where do you want to be in five/ten/twenty years' time? *This is a self-esteem issue!* Regard this as important enough to find out and start today, even in the 30 minutes you have to reflect on this.

What do you want to achieve? What would you hate not to achieve? Bring in self-esteem and personal intuition to keep discovering what is appropriate for you so you can set goals and take action. Bring in self-esteem at all times for self-motivation, to get started, to persevere and complete each stage of your exciting journey.

Self-esteem boosters

- Brush up skills you want to improve, for example for interviews or having a greater facility with IT.
- Support your success by keeping self-esteem thoughts to the forefront of your mind like 'I can do this', 'I'm building on the success I already have', 'I now deserve to have work I love'.
- Back up your self-esteem thoughts by letting go of any feelings of self-blame or blaming others.
- Consider further training. Is that going to be necessary? Find out!
- Expand the network of people who know you're in the job market. Consider attending meetings of professional

associations, conferences, local business associations as well as telling friends, family, colleagues and former colleagues.

■ Have this as your most important project, *the right work for you*. Keep notes daily of your ideas and practical steps to take.

Keynote booster

Keynote boosters can be used for a day or more, then use another booster of your choice.

Take a minute ... several times today to reflect both on how you can improve your current job situation and on how you can move towards the ideal work for *you*.

9

SELF-ESTEEM TREATMENT

Pay Attention To What You Need

Look after yourself

You boost your self-esteem by paying attention to what you need to do to keep yourself feeling good. Because it is your responsibility to do this, not another person's, that puts you in a position of *power and independence*. It also means you don't blame others or any other person in particular for your feeling bad, low self-esteem or out of sorts with yourself!

While you won't want to accept behaviour that's rude or inappropriate, you don't need other people to behave in a certain way so that you may feel good. Now that's a relief. What freedom for them and for you, what a self-esteem boost!

Treating yourself better – what can you do?

Treating yourself well does include being vigilant with regard to your mind, not allowing yourself to focus on thoughts that are hurtful or irrelevant to you. It's also not wasting your time on things that are not important. You can use your time on matters that are important to you, yet in a way that's enjoyable. You might want to stop and ask yourself right now 'What is the most important use of my time today?'

Self-esteem treatment is caring for yourself on all levels. With regard to your body, it may be giving yourself enough rest and relaxation, enough exercise, grooming, nice coloured clothes or treatments, foods that nurture you and that you enjoy eating. You've got to eat, dress and groom yourself anyway so it may just as easily be in a way that enhances your self-esteem as not!

What self-esteem treatment can you give your body this week? You may be able to think of several. However, spending 15–30 minutes on something this week may be more satisfying than a longer time further into the future, helping you to start now to treat your body well. Then look at treating yourself better in other ways.

- Can you treat yourself better with regard to enhancing your closest relationship? Can you make that more intimate and romantic or whatever it is you want for yourself?
- With regard to friends and family, have you got the balance of those who are supportive, with those who you spend a great deal of time supporting? Are there people you'd love to spend time with? When can you make arrangements?
- With regard to treating yourself better in terms of your home or work environment, are there ways you can

improve that, make it more pleasurable by keeping things tidy, bringing in more fresh flowers, plants and pictures?

Self-esteem treatment is looking after yourself in all aspects. It's particularly important to treat yourself gently when the pressure is on. Be aware that treating yourself well from a self-esteem point of view goes beyond indulging yourself or giving yourself treats.

Your deeper needs

Looking after yourself, treating yourself well, is not just caring for your immediate physical and personality needs. You will always have more desires: that is part of the mechanism that moves us forward. To treat yourself really well, from a self-esteem perspective, you need to pay attention to your deeper needs which will be personal to you as an individual.

Sometimes satisfaction comes from working later to complete a project or piece of work that is important to you. At other times it comes from stopping work early to do something completely different. Only you can decide this for yourself.

Find out what is joyful and important to you

What is important to you and what gives you joy may be very different from what is appropriate for any other person. It can also take you time to find out what is important for you to accomplish long term as well as on a daily basis. You may also need to reflect on what gives you joy. This is very personal to you and may vary from time to time. *Respecting yourself in this way will provide a lasting boost to your self-esteem.*

Self-esteem boosters

- Think of one way you could do something that gives you joy, that's pleasing to you and make the time to do it.
- Don't torture or hurt yourself by saying or thinking 'unkind' things about yourself or others. Let go and focus on what you now want to create in your life.
- Listen to yourself, to how you are feeling. Do what is necessary to get your body feeling good and your energy higher.
- Treat yourself well with regard to how you spend your time and energy, daily and long term. Think of one way you can treat yourself better in each area of your life and make plans to put that in place.

Keynote booster

Keynote boosters can be used for a day or more, then use another booster of your choice.

Take a minute ... several times today to ask 'What can I do for myself this week that is enjoyable?' Put a date and a time in your diary to do it.

10

SET GOALS WITH SELF-ESTEEM

For Plans You Really Follow Through

Wake up to what you want

Low self-esteem is tied in with low aspirations. This is when you have no significantly important goals for yourself on a professional or a personal basis. With a boosted level of self-esteem it may be time to wake up and consider what you do want for yourself! It can be a vicious circle. Because of low self-esteem, you don't think or feel that you're worthy or capable of achieving or receiving very much. So you don't set goals that are important and meaningful to you. There follows dissatisfaction and further low self-esteem!

The cycle continues until you do decide to boost your self-esteem by choosing helpful thoughts, by caring for and respecting yourself enough to listen to yourself. This is with regard to what is important to *you* and joyful for you to achieve.

You know what is best for *you*

Having the self-esteem to listen to yourself includes giving attention and time to consider your hunches with regard to goals that are right for *you*. It means that you listen to yourself with regard to steps that are appropriate for you to take. It is this listening to the whispers in your mind, to elements of your dreams and daydreams, to your hunches, as well as having a relaxed yet alert consideration of what it is appropriate for you at any time. Reflecting on choices from a point of self-esteem is more likely to lead you to goals that will be truly satisfying and that you will want to follow through.

The right goals for you

So take a few minutes to pay attention to this daily or at least on a regular basis. Then you can formulate goals for things you truly want to achieve. While you will wish to bring into the picture, or even better, set mutual goals with friends, family and colleagues, you won't want, through low self-esteem, to take on the 'shoulds' of other people. For high self-esteem you need to put your time and energy into what you as an individual want to achieve. This is for both your long-term goals and daily objectives.

Outline the vital or essential aspects of your goal, or goals. For example, if you want to reorganize your garden and the most important thing is to have fragrance and vegetables, then work in the relevant parts first.

If you want a new job, look at exactly which aspects are most important. For some people, location will be a primary consideration. Others need to have plenty of people around them or the opportunity to use their creative skills.

Deciding what you want

Work out what is appropriate for you. If you want more fun, what does that mean to you? This can vary enormously from one person to another!

Obviously some goals will be easier to achieve than others. Write out goals as clearly as you can, putting in a time frame – one year, six months, three months, one month, one week, or whatever you choose. What do you have as your most important goal for yourself through the next year, six, or three months? If it's a job, for example, you may want to be settled in a new one and to have set up appropriate training within a year. You may want to have set up interviews within six months. You may want to have clarified exactly what you want within three months or even one month. You can speed up the time frame to fit in with what you want.

Self-esteem supports your success

When you're focusing on what is appropriate to you, another thing to remember are your self-esteem thoughts. You need to have appropriate thoughts as well as setting goals. There's no point in having goals you want for yourself and then telling yourself, 'I'll never manage to do this', 'I'm not good enough'. Change your thoughts to 'I am good enough to do this', 'I'm making progress'. From a self-esteem angle, think about who will be supportive of you, someone or more than one person who has your best interests at heart or who has just achieved what you want to do or who simply can be of professional assistance to you. Then just reflect on practical steps you need to take. Planning one of them as something you can do in the next week means that you take a first step right away.

Unless you give yourself what you really want at a deep

level, dissatisfaction, resentment and low self-esteem will continue. Rather than goals you feel you 'should' have, goals that are dear to your heart, important to you as an individual, will be the goals that you will want to follow through.

Self-esteem boosters

■ Listen to yourself and then keep a note of hunches, dreams, ideas and thoughts on your project.

■ Write out your goals clearly with time frames, perhaps one year, six months, three months and one month.

■ Add self-esteem thoughts to support your goals, for example 'I know what I want to achieve', 'I can do this', then use your own most helpful thoughts.

■ Look at what needs to be changed or improved. Make a step-by-step plan to tackle this.

■ Who will support you? Are there people who can be supportive of you in achieving this goal?

■ What is a step you can take right now to move forward?

■ Review your goals, spending a short time on them each week. Take one at a time, then even a few minutes planning will be well spent.

Keynote booster

Keynote boosters can be used for a day or more, then use another booster of your choice.

Take a minute ... several times today to ask yourself of different activities – 'How does this fit in with today's most important goal for myself?'

'PICK ME UP' PAGE

However well prepared and confident we are, there will always be people and situations that tend to throw us. All you have learnt in the book will help you to deal with the strong emotions you may experience. However, for a quick boost in a crisis:

- Take a deep breath, relax your body, remind yourself 'I can handle this'.
- Get away from the situation or person on your own if you can, even for a short time. This may mean walking around the block or at least to the loo if that's at work.
- Experience your feelings and let them go. If you can't do this now because you're at work, set aside a time later when you know you will do this and keep to it.
- Bring in self-esteem thoughts, supportive thoughts about yourself and the situation, for example 'I can handle this'/'I believe in myself'.
- Talk to someone you trust to get it out of your system or write it out.
- As you relax a little and centre yourself, become aware of what's the most appropriate step for you to take.
- Remind yourself this is a situation that you're *going through* and you will come through it!

- Do something enjoyable for yourself today to give yourself a break from the situation.
- Keep letting go and bringing in self-esteem thoughts.
- Listen to yourself with regard to appropriate steps and get support from friends on this.

FINALE

Boosting your self-esteem is about getting back in balance, having all aspects of your life work together for you. Self-esteem thoughts with appropriate actions give you more joy and satisfaction in your life. Self-esteem on an emotional level works by your letting yourself feel your feelings, whatever they are, so that they change and flow, then you're not stuck with your anger, resentment and fear. It also works when you bring in feelings of having everything working out well. Remember, you can bring in those good feelings when you choose.

It's very important to have that 15 minutes of time just for you each day, however you want to use it, so long as it's something you enjoy. It's space and time for you. People report greater self-esteem and satisfaction when they give themselves even a small amount of time, especially when they're very busy. By satisfying the 'what about me?' part of you, you're satisfying yourself. Then you're more likely to want to satisfy other people, which is particularly important with regard to work colleagues and customers.

While you can continue your self-esteem building further through programmes – either public or for your organization – you already have the basis for boosting your self-esteem whenever you want to use it.

Perhaps the biggest boost to your self-esteem is knowing that you *can* boost your own self-esteem! Then while you may be apparently 'dependent' on other people for some of the material aspects of your life and, with regard to work, if you have a boss to 'answer' to, you will still have *inner independence*. This in itself makes the process valuable and worthwhile.

Once you've read this book through and put those suggestions that appeal to you into practice, you'll have a greater sense of *strength* and *freedom* as a result of *boosting your self-esteem*.

Take a minute ... or even 30, to look at what you now want for yourself and in your life. Believe in yourself. You can do it. You have the rest of your life ahead of you. With higher self-esteem so much more is possible!

FURTHER INFORMATION

If you would like to find out more about Patricia Cleghorn's work, you may be interested in programmes by Orchid International, for people in organizations and The Self-Esteem Company, with courses for the public. Please contact:

Patricia Cleghorn, Principal
Orchid International, The Self-Esteem Company
PO Box 354
London, W13 9NU
Tel: 44 (0)1491 875135
email: orchid2100@aol.com

30 Minutes
...To Get Promoted

DIANA CAMBRIDGE

KOGAN PAGE

Kogan Page Limited
120 Pentonville Road
London N1 9JN

British Library Cataloguing in Publication Data
A CIP record for this book is available from the British Library.

ISBN 0 7494 3315 9

Typeset by Florence Production Ltd, Stoodleigh, Devon

Printed and bound in Great Britain by Clays Ltd, St Ives plc

CONTENTS

Contents

The 30 Minutes Series

Titles available are: *30 Minutes* . . .

Before a Meeting

Before a Presentation

Before Your Job Appraisal

Before Your Job Interview

To Boost Your Communication Skills

To Boost Your Self-Esteem

To Brainstorm Great Ideas

To Deal with Difficult People

To Get Your Own Way

To Get Yourself Promoted

To Improve Telesales Techniques

To Make the Right Decision

To Make the Right Impression

To Make Yourself Richer

To Manage Information Overload

To Manage Your Time Better

To Market Yourself

To Master the Internet

To Motivate Your Staff

To Negotiate a Better Deal

To Plan a Project

To Prepare a Job Application

To Solve That Problem

To Succeed in Business Writing

To Understand the Financial Pages

To Write a Business Plan

To Write a Marketing Plan

To Write a Report

To Write Sales Letters

Available from all good booksellers.
For further information on the series, please contact:

Kogan Page, 120 Pentonville Road, London N1 9JN
Tel: 020 7278 0433 Fax: 020 7837 6348

www.kogan-page.co.uk

INTRODUCTION

We spend most of our lives working but put a small percentage of our effort into actively engineering our promotion. We tend to think of promotion as luck or fate or something that happens to other, more talented people. In fact there are techniques and tricks of the trade you can follow to climb up the management ladder.

You can get yourself selected for advancement (and earn more money) by taking on more responsibility and making a commitment to your immediate boss. Spending, say, half an hour a day doing extra things for your line manager will accelerate your promotion chances. One extra half day every six weeks doing your admin, and thinking up small cost-cutting and efficiency plans and ideas for new business will be a great asset to you.

Consider these two examples: a shoe shop assistant had the idea of colour-coding shoe boxes with tiny stars so that assistants could immediately pick out the right sizes. A junior manager in a DIY firm offered to build the company's Web site. Both ideas speeded up work, helped customers and staff, increased sales and were cheap to carry out. Within a year both employees had been promoted.

Turn every setback into success for you with your secret promotion plan. In Mrs Thatcher's famous words, bring solutions not problems to your place of work! By making the most of your energy and perseverance your chances of moving up and earning more money are enhanced 100 per cent.

Promotion isn't necessarily based on talent, but more on your approach to work, and your staying power. There are talented employees who become disenchanted, bored or feel they're under-valued. They get irritable and 'difficult'. Some start to take days off. If you put your energy into your 'promotion plan' even when you feel tired or bored, you'll definitely be rewarded.

You can begin your promotion plan at any time. Why not start today?

1

THINK SUCCESS

If you want promotion, begin your strategy today. Promotion begins not with qualifications on paper, but with what's in your mind. Commitment to yourself, your career plan and to your immediate boss is essential. Make yourself indispensable to your boss – take work off his or her hands, do it well and do it quietly.

You need to develop a strong work ethic, but the good news is you don't have to work day and night. Just working an extra half an hour every day on projects for your immediate boss will enhance your promotion prospects. Even if you have already been promoted, you can't count on further promotion being automatic: you still need to work at it. It's essential to keep up the momentum, even if at times you feel like quitting.

Written goals are always more effective than goals stored in your mind. You need to begin by putting your current goals in writing, maybe in a special notebook. Write down: your career goal for the next five years, your goal for the next six months and two small projects that you can plan and implement in the next three months. These goals and projects might be ideas for encouraging more customers to open accounts, or a simple plan for making things easier to find in the stock room. Perhaps you have ideas about cutting costs in your department, or about a team-building strategy you could manage, or you want to create a Web site for your company. Write these projects and goals down and you will have the key part of your career plan.

TIP

Don't worry if you haven't got a degree, an MBA or whatever. What counts towards promotion is how you perform at work.

No one gets promoted with a nine-to-five mentality. You have to do more. Keep setting goals.

These are the five essential qualities that bosses look for in people they promote:

- reliability – always meeting deadlines and having a good attendance record;
- trustworthiness;
- willingness to accept responsibility;
- productivity;
- cheerfulness.

To this list you can add integrity – bosses need to count on their staff not passing on company secrets, dabbling in insider share dealing or risking the company's reputation by being drunk or taking drugs at work.

There are other important qualities you need to develop for your promotion kitbag:

- always be courteous;
- smile often;
- look smart;
- pass on helpful tips to colleagues;
- don't sulk or bear grudges;
- answer the phone with a welcoming voice.

Media bosses on a recruitment course defined their best daily newspaper editors as well groomed, ever-courteous, with a 'radiant' welcoming smile at all times. The men and women they singled out for promotion worked long hours when necessary, always had time for other staff members, were sociable and showed a sense of humour. Though most had an editorial background, they were also aware of the total picture – not just within their own newspapers, but the entire newspaper group. They took personal responsibility for learning all they could about budget control, advertising, sales and managing people.

A charming manner and good appearance are things you can cultivate and work at – you don't have to be born with them. In today's business arena, social skills are as crucial as vocational skills. Someone whose ideal job is one where he or she hides away most of the time (and that used to include many bosses) is unlikely to be suitable for promotion. You need to be interested in the entire company, not just your bit of it, and that means teaching yourself as well as going on courses. You teach yourself by networking to become more informed and spending time with colleagues from different departments.

Warning: try to never lose control in the office. For men this means not losing your temper and swearing at someone, for women it means not crying. If you ever feel upset and out of control (and everyone does sometimes) leave the office for ten minutes and walk about outside or have a coffee. You will be able to return feeling more poised.

TIP

Leaders reach people on an emotional level, as well as through their management skills.

Looking good for work

Doing well at work begins the moment you wake up! How organized is your morning routine? You can begin to 'think' your way into a new role using time management. Set your alarm for half an hour earlier than you need. Then you'll have time to pay attention to your appearance. Use uplifting bath oils and splash colognes to get you going.

Try to look reasonably good every day, rather than fantastic sometimes and a slob at others. Invest in haircuts and shoes – spend as much as you can afford on these two items and the rest of your outfit needn't be expensive. However, an expensive briefcase will always enhance your image.

Looking youthful is an asset, which can be annoying for older people. Short grey hair looks fine but men and women should avoid having straggling grey locks!

TIP

Women should always wear some make-up to work: they always look more confident and professional with a little make-up rather than barefaced.

Feeling good

First, don't skip breakfast. Eat or drink something early on that will energize you. Try *Get up and Go!* – a vitamin-packed powder breakfast drink you mix with juice (available by mail order from sales@highernature.co.uk).

Visualize yourself in your new role: spend five minutes every day just seeing yourself, strongly, as you'll be when you're promoted. Shut your eyes and focus on you, smiling, forceful and confident in your new role. The more you reinforce your vision of promotion, the more you're likely to succeed.

TIP

Hands and teeth are noticed at work — take care of yours.

Wear deodorant at work – BO is offensive and would probably spoil your chances of promotion.

Fitting into the office culture

It's essential to fit into the office culture if you want to be promoted. Bosses look for people who:

- are clubbable;
- have a good network of contacts;
- show a sense of humour.

This means you do need to be able to socialize a bit. Don't be tempted to skip staff or floor meetings. If they're followed by a get-together in or out of the office, have at least one drink. If you feel shy, join a group near your manager. Lots of people avoid office socializing and tend to rush home. But if you want to get on, you do need to join in with the office culture. This includes bringing in cream cakes or standing a round of drinks when it's your birthday, having a night out twice a year with the people you work with or just attending the office bash at Christmas. It doesn't matter what it is – but you need to be there.

Communicating by e-mail

Put quality into all your office communication (including e-mail): make it courteous, prompt and helpful.

E-mail etiquette

When using e-mail:

- add the word 'thanks' to every request you make;
- don't write in capital letters;
- never be rude or sarcastic by e-mail;
- complete the conversation – send back a quick 'That's great, thanks' or 'Will do' or whatever's needed to complete the exchange;
- answer all e-mails within the day or as promptly as possible.

Begin to dress, behave and communicate the way a manager would – and start today.

Useful Web site for international seminars and private coaching on business goal-setting, health and fitness: **www.bright-idea.co.uk**

2

CHARACTER BUILDING

You already have the character traits that qualify you for promotion or you wouldn't be reading this book. But although the promotion path begins in the mind, those around you, especially your managers, are not mind-readers, so you have to demonstrate your ability.

Personal development

As you increase your personal power and strength, enhance your skills and stay focused, you will enjoy your own personal development. You will know you're moving towards your goal. One of the messages of this book is that life needn't be dull just because you intend to be promoted, but the discipline to persevere, to keep on reaching for goals despite setbacks, is a vital asset. Consider this example: a woman was promoted because she set herself the task of opening more customer accounts. All she did was ask every customer she served whether they'd like to open a credit account. Every assistant in the shop was asked to do the same, and they even got a small commission for each account opened. But the majority of sales assistants got fed-up after a few failures and abandoned card enquiries. The woman who kept going (who incidentally had left college with no qualifications) was noticed and promoted to 'motivator', encouraging co-workers to open more customer accounts. Within 18 months she was promoted to deputy floor manager.

Your behaviour while pursuing your goals is important. Don't complain; especially about things you could put right yourself. Be the one to fill up the photocopier with paper or untangle the fax machine. Be reliable: always meet deadlines. Don't get tangled up in office cliques.

Starting a romance

Try to keep your love life separate from your business life. Successful romances can begin at work, but starting them is risky. If the relationship goes wrong you'll feel very uncomfortable and you or the other person involved might even have to leave the company.

TIP

Three tips on keeping an office flirtation just that:

- Don't see the office party as a romantic arena – stay in a group, have fun, then leave early.
- Don't get involved in a steamy e-mail romance with a colleague.
- Do keep focused on your career aims.

Age is no barrier

If you're a mature employee – let's say over 45 years old – your age should not be a handicap to taking on increased responsibility and getting promoted, it should be an asset, so don't be ageist about yourself. Provided you have a cheerful, youthful, disciplined outlook, a sense of humour and can get on with younger colleagues, your maturity will not stand in your way at all.

The company could have 10 or 15 years of good work from you – probably more than from young people who tend to move jobs in the early years. Plus, you have both work and life experience and, if you were educated pre-1970s, your literacy skills may be far superior to those of youngsters. If you've brought up a family, you have practical skills and responsibility which young people may lack. But you do have to fit into today's workplace, which is much less formal, busier and more flexible than it was 20 years ago. Flexibility is the key word for your promotion prospects.

Dealing with the office environment

Try to put up with and adapt to any minor irritations in your office. If you find the office noisy, use earphones rather than complain; if it's too hot or too cold, dress accordingly. This can mean wearing summer clothes in winter, and vice versa at the office. Today's offices tend to be cramped and noisy, but one good thing about career progress is that as you move up, you often get more space!

> ### TIP
>
> A generally cheerful voice and manner is an asset. Use a sarcastic or ironic tone too often and people will be wary of you, and find you unapproachable (which is a disadvantage if you're aiming for promotion). It's good to see the funny side of work life and be able to lighten the atmosphere with a joke.

Coping with nerves

If you want to move up in the company, your voice needs to be heard. But you don't have to be a super-confident orator, or a chatterbox. Do speak up at meetings, making at least one contribution, even if you're basically shy. The more you do this, the less reserved you'll be.

If you're worried about how your voice sounds – maybe you think it sounds too quiet or too posh or too high – invest in some voice training. Ring a local dance and theatre school to see if they have voice projection classes. Look in *Yellow Pages* under Speech and Drama Tutors, many of them specialize in coaching businesspeople. You can also source acting lessons (through acting schools) for businesspeople.

Body language is important, but mainly to convey an impression of energy and alertness. Move around the office

> ### TIP
>
> Nervous before going into a meeting? Try clenching everything – buttocks, chest and jaw – before you step through the door. As you release, you'll feel instantly relaxed.

briskly and purposefully – no slouching or putting your head down on your desk.

Work at home

Willingness to do extra work at home is a characteristic of someone who will be promoted. Think of the work you do at home as a pleasure and not a chore. You can use the time to study reports in a more detailed way, draft ideas and letters and bone up on the training manual.

Home practicals

It's useful to have:

- A computer at home so that you can do some work in your spare time on floppy disks and send e-mails.
- A year planner with deadlines marked in red.
- Colourful ring binders in which you can keep memos, notes from your boss and your replies. Every time you get a piece of paper, a chart or memo you don't want to lose, add it to your file. This becomes your 'work-book' and you can easily take it home.
- Coloured 'Post-Its' at work and at home to remind you of items and phone numbers you might need.

TIP

Don't fall into the 'comfort trap' at work. If it becomes too easy and comfortable, you'll lose the incentive to move on up and after a while you'll become bored. Aim to be resourceful. If you keep taking opportunities your work life will always offer challenge.

Useful Web site: heading to 50 and seeking promotion? The *I Don't Feel Fifty* site at **www.idf50.co.uk/home.asp** has informative features for older people on topics ranging from health to work.

3

GO A BIT FURTHER

The person who gets promoted is the one who goes that bit further. Don't just wait to carry out instructions, but suggest ideas for improving the business, for getting new clients or changing the way something is done. Take all the training you can, including courses in your spare time. People chasing promotion do not make personal phone calls, gossip or chat when there's a lull in workload. Instead they do things that will move the company on. They're constantly busy and productive, turning out quality work.

If there's something you enjoy doing which you have a talent for, suggest in writing to your line manager that you take it on. It could be any of the following:

- doing some PR for your company;
- dealing with customer complaints;
- using your second language to increase business;
- coaching beginners in telephone skills;
- sorting out records that everyone else has found a reason not to tackle;

- arranging training courses;
- helping work-experience trainees to settle in.

Someone has to do all these jobs and, particularly in a small company, anyone willing to tackle them on top of their own work will be valued.

Keep learning

Maybe there's a part of your work that worries you – perhaps giving presentations or dealing with some aspect of new technology. It's a good idea to buy in your own training. If you choose a private coach the investment will be worth it for the increased confidence. Alternatively, look in *Yellow Pages* for your local further education college. Larger colleges offer a range of part-time business courses (including many dealing with information technology and with presentation skills).

If your own firm offers training, take advantage of it. Companies often find that they have spare places on some courses because employees find reasons to drop out more often than attend. So it's worth putting your name down for last-minute cancellations. If your company has training manuals, work steadily through them.

If there's something special you'd like to learn, ask your manager whether the firm will fund training. Don't be downcast if your request is refused, it just means that, like all companies, yours has to cut costs and may even have a freeze on outside training. Be resourceful – see if you can do a modified version of the training yourself, perhaps by buying a book and video on it.

One form of coaching you might like to consider is NLP (Neuro-Linguistic Programming). This is a well-respected business and sales tool and especially useful to help you with the perseverance and staying power you need for promotion.

NLP can help you to:

- think 'strong';
- turn negative thoughts into positive ones;
- set goals and reach them;
- develop instant rapport with others;
- be more persuasive;
- achieve excellence in work.

Be your own PA

Good word-processing skills are important for any top job. Today's bosses don't expect to have a team of secretaries and personal assistants. Many managers prepare all their own letters, reports and presentations: they may have a shared secretary but that job will mainly involve organization, not copy typing.

The more you can be your own PA, the more useful you will be to the firm. Knowing how to perform simple tasks like attaching a new mouse or cleaning an old one, or unblocking a jammed photocopier, for example, are all extremely useful.

TIP

Learn how to do spreadsheets – if you want to be a manager this is a great asset.

Check, check and check your work again. Make proof-reading all your work second nature.

Employees with fast, excellent word-processing and computer skills are sought after as managers because they bring added value to the company.

It's worth learning about e-mail and the Internet, and how to write for the Web. You could be even more of an asset to your company if you acquire some desktop publishing skills (perhaps in Quark or Aldus Pagemaker). Many companies want to produce materials in house, such as publicity newsletters, magazines, shoppers' lists, or press releases.

Sales success

> ### TIP
>
> Aim to have a mix of both creative and commercial skills.
>
> Could you build a Web site? If you could, and you work in a small company and seek promotion, offer this.

As more and more retailers combine, opportunities in customer sales are increasing: retailers are constantly looking for employees willing and able to both manage other people and sell goods. In shops, if you're able to go that bit further, to supervise and sell, your career will flourish. Look towards this dual role for promotion.

Seven career tips for super sales assistants:

1. Offer ideas to increase sales.
2. Keep a vigilant eye on shop security (reducing shop-lifting is a major part of some retail work).
3. Help colleagues with problems.
4. Coach new staff in selling and in using the tills.
5. Stay late without complaint.
6. Smile at every customer.
7. Think of new ways of keeping the stockroom tidy.

If you work in a small shop, and have started as a junior sales assistant, simply by following these seven tips to seize more and more responsibility you could be shop manager within a couple of years. If you already manage a small shop, take an interest in the wider picture: ask if you can visit other branches, attend conferences or receive copies of appropriate reports.

TIP

If you work in a shop, keep thinking of 'add-ons' your shop could offer. What would customers who use your services also be interested in?

Play the game

If you have to take part in business games or role-playing try to join in cheerfully even if you don't enjoy it. After all, it's just a few hours out of your life. Many companies now value 'fulfil your own potential' workshops – and fulfilling your own potential may mean punching a piece of wood, standing on a chair or doing something that seems equally daft. Unfortunately you will have to grit your teeth and bear it. If you're honest, announce that the whole thing seems a waste of time and you're not going to do it, your chances of promotion will rapidly decrease.

TIP

Aim to be stoic and get through something you dislike, such as a course where you have to make a fool of yourself or join in a silly game. Refuseniks dig their own career graves!

Stay the course

Staying power is vital if you want promotion. It's more important than talent. Many of us begin a new job well and can be earmarked as achievers. Yet when the adrenaline of the new job wears off and a few difficulties, or difficult people, have to be tackled, that first sparkle can wane.

You can mark yourself out as promotion-worthy just by keeping up the enthusiasm despite any setbacks. Try to be at your 'interview best' as often as you can. The more you can keep this up, the easier it gets. Being able to react positively is a learned skill, and gets easier with practice.

TIP

Keep acting as if you have that desired promotion. It won't be instant, but the pay-off will come.

Work on your staying power as well as than your 'first impression' persona. Don't beat yourself up emotionally if you do have 'off days' – just don't have too many!

Useful Web site for more information on NLP courses: **www.nlp-community.com**

4

YOU AND
YOUR BOSS

You'll go a long way with your boss if you make a personal, private commitment to putting his or her work first. Commit strongly and respond well again and again to requests that other workers grumble about. Be the one who never has to be e-mailed a second time or reminded about reports, admin or sales charts.

Always give priority to whatever your boss asks and try to turn it around in 24 hours, even if it means working late. An extra half an hour spent daily on just your boss's requests will reward you well. Most people will leave stuff from the boss to the last minute, resenting it all the way. Try to get work to your manager well ahead of time – be the first in with it!

Open all you boss's e-mails first and respond to them promptly. Make your replies brief. When things in the office are stressful, a touch of humour is often appreciated. Try not to knock on your manager's door to ask for advice or meetings. Think in terms of saving his or her time. Verbal communication takes up time, so instead of communicating ideas, suggestions or responses verbally, put things in writing.

Always deliver what you say you'll deliver, but do not expect 'stroking' for work done quickly and well. Bosses value highly employees who consistently meet high targets but who don't crave applause. The payback will come later. The responsibility for maintaining a good relationship with you boss lies with you, not with him or her.

TIP

Never use the word 'try' to your boss, as in 'I'll try to have that report in by tomorrow at five o'clock'. Your reply is always 'I'll have it ready by five o'clock tomorrow'.

Welcome routine chores

Be on top of your admin. If you hate doing forms, accounts or timesheets and are often late with them, schedule in one morning every six weeks when you can concentrate on them in 'out of work' hours. At first it will seem tedious, but you'll be surprised how productive you can be when you concentrate on just admin. Often admin seems boring – well, it often is boring – but your boss has the even worse job of collating it. Chasing up consistent late-comers is an extra burden for a manager. No matter how good you are at the creative side of work, low-grade admin gives you a black mark. Think of each bit of boring admin successfully completed as another step towards that promotion.

TIP

Always make your boss look good. If group hostility seems to be directed at him or her, say something to lighten the atmosphere or offer your boss support. Don't be afraid of being singled out by colleagues as the boss's pet. Colleagues won't promote you; your boss will!

Develop your relationship with your boss

Chemistry between you and your boss is important. But this is created over time, not overnight. So don't worry if things are not immediately easy between you. By your solid hard work and loyalty you'll create a rapport. You can improve the rapport by 'mirroring': if your boss tends to speak slowly and carefully, adopt a similar style; if he or she is a fast talker with a strong sense of humor,

TIP

Companies don't promote 'yes-men' – it's a short-term gain. So although a junior manager may appear to always agree with the boss, you can bet that in private they have disagreements, with the junior manager finding fault (politely) in the top manager's plan. By now they will know each other quite well. Bosses want managers who are strong, not weak.

Never gossip to colleagues about your boss.

Never pass on information your boss gives you.

reflect that. If your boss reacts to problems with a joke rather than agonizing, adopt this light-hearted response up to a point but remember he or she is still taking it very seriously. If you have a more earnest boss who tends not to make many jokes, follow that example. Mirroring is a question of tact and common sense – you can still be yourself.

If your boss asks you to lunch or for a drink, that's a good sign. But always remember you're still at work: even if your boss is around your age and similar to you in style, don't imagine he or she is going to be your best friend. If your boss talks about personal matters such as holidays, family or home, respond with interest. One thing your boss will never do – or shouldn't do – is criticize his or her own boss to you, so that's something you never think of doing.

Let your manager introduce work topics, and follow the lead. Think of it as a 'working lunch' or 'working drink' rather than a social occasion. Be enthusiastic and optimistic about work topics, welcoming any change he or she suggests. At the end of each social encounter your boss will think of you as a positive and helpful person, an asset to the company. But don't ask 'How am I doing?' or 'Am I doing OK?' over a drink or snack – keep that kind of feedback for your appraisal.

Your boss will value your view 'from the floor'. Never gossip about or rubbish fellow workers. But you can relay to him the 'mood' of your department or details of any procedures that seem to need changing. Be honest and unemotional here as the boss may get enough resentment and whingeing from other workers. Always be positive, for example: 'I think it will take people a little while to get used to the new Internet ordering system, but it could work very well.'

Your boss may seem friendly – remember he or she has been promoted partly because of social skills – but he or she won't become a close friend now because a boss's commitment is to the company and the career it offers, not to individuals within it. Aim to be your boss's helpful aide: someone to be trusted and relied upon. This is the role your boss plays to his or her boss.

TIP

At a lunch or drinks session, your boss is the main player. Don't try to set the agenda. Let your boss introduce topics, invite comments, set the tone – and pay the bill! You should offer politely to pay your way, but he or she won't let you. Never insist on paying for yourself.

Useful Web site for advice on better working relationships: **www.qsilvertlc.com**

5

WORKING
WITH OTHERS

Aiming for promotion does not mean being a toady. Employers look for team players who gain respect from colleagues, have persuasive skills and can see ideas from different points of view. Managers promote people with the strength of character to tell them, politely and in private, that their idea for selling electric blankets in Saudi Arabia is crazy – and suggesting one or two more promising ideas.

Once a decision has been taken, however, managers want you to support it when they sell it to the staff. People resist change and come up with many reasons for disliking a new idea. You need the courage to be the one who says it's worth a try or that though it may seem cumbersome at first, it will be more efficient in the long run. Expect your promotion chances to be weakened if you join in with the general 'We don't want it' response to change. You have to be flexible and prepared to welcome change now.

Difficult people

Often doing well at work isn't just a matter of the actual work, but of dealing with the people you work with. If only they were all the same as you. But they're not, and some of them will definitely be difficult. Difficult people are always there and working with someone you dislike is unavoidable. If we all refused to work with people we didn't like, most of the businesses in the country would come to a standstill.

How will you cope with a prickly or unco-operative colleague? It may be that this person isn't really dreadful but just different in personality to you. He or she may be more assertive, extrovert, even a touch aggressive. You have to get on with him or her if you're to get things done. This person is unlikely to change, so if you want promotion, accept the responsibility for making this tricky relationship work.

You need to accept that it isn't necessary to like everyone at work, or for them to like you. Fit in with nuisance people, so that they have no complaints about your work. Don't try to become friends or seek out these people's company, all that's needed is that you 'rub along' at work. Be pleasant and neutral even when they are a pain: don't try to get them to like you.

Four tips for dealing with awkward people:

- don't respond to annoying remarks;

- don't get involved in their petty disputes;

- don't make an official complaint;

- remember it won't just be you who finds someone troublesome – difficult people are generally unpopular.

TIP

Never waste time worrying about what people are saying about you – there's nothing you can do about it. It really doesn't matter. The higher up you go, the more people will talk about you. And it still doesn't matter! If you want promotion, think strong and develop a thicker skin.

Chat attacks

Another problem can be working with someone you like! If you find that chatting and laughing with a colleague you like distracts you from work, you may need to do something about it. Your friend may not be as promotion-hungry as you are – so what do you do? You don't want to spoil the friendship, but you do want to focus on your work. Again you'll have to take the responsibility for keeping the friendship manageable. Try to move the friendship to the after-hours part of your life, keeping office time free to promote your career.

When your friend starts chatting on Monday morning, say 'Yes, I've got loads to tell you. Shall we have a drink after work tomorrow?'. Arrange to have lunch together once a week, or do a course or go to the gym together so you have a regular date.

Perhaps you sit near your friend. Try moving your seat away slightly so you aren't quite so vulnerable to chat attacks. But make the move seem natural. Don't upset your friend – people you really get on with are essential allies.

> ## TIP
>
> If you have children, don't go on about them in the office. Workers who do this are seen as less ambitious and less motivated.

Be a tactful teacher

You may have to check other people's work in your job. The better you are at coaching and supervising, the more you enhance your promotion prospects. If someone has done a job that still needs some revision, tactful ways of asking for amendments are:

'It's fine – it just needs a few tweaks here and there.'

'I've had a look at it and it looks great. But we need a bit more detail on these few points…'

Always thank other people for the work they've done. Always give tips and advice that will help them amend the work and advance their skills.

> ## TIP
>
> Bosses look for people who can coach and check without being resented. Aim to be relaxed, courteous and helpful, and learn to see yourself as coaching rather than correcting.
>
> People who can 'finish' (check details, chase deadlines and ensure the process is completed) are sought after by bosses. But the nature of the task can mean being unpopular in the office. Don't let this put you off.

> ### TIP
>
> Treat all situations and people with integrity. Don't be nicer to people you like – or at least not in the office!
>
> Be fair. In a small meeting, it shouldn't be only your voice which is heard, other people should also speak.

Listen – don't talk

Listening skills are very valuable and you can acquire them. The best managers are always great listeners. They let you speak while they listen carefully. You'll often find in a one-to-one situation these managers don't say much at all, but just by listening to you they make you feel better, valued, understood. The trick they have learnt is to let the other person talk, so use this trick yourself with co-workers. Don't interrupt or rush in with advice.

Seven ways to get on better with co-workers:

- handle people's feelings carefully;
- share a drink now and then with colleagues;
- be kind if someone feels unwell: see if they can go early;
- don't ring colleagues at home to ask why they're away;
- make coffee for fellow workers;
- coach – if someone's struggling with a task, help them;
- never make fun of people for not understanding something.

Support others

Colleagues are sometimes surprisingly poor at supporting each other in times of trouble. 'I just didn't know what to say' is a common reaction to someone else's bad fortune. If a colleague is made redundant, or suffers serious illness, for example, put something in writing to them. A brief note or card saying you're sorry it should happen to them is always appreciated.

If someone asks you for a reference or for advice on their own career, respond promptly. Try to respond to these requests in 24 hours as they're very important to people. If you can do this, you'll get pay-off later. When you are promoted, you'll find you already have a platform of loyalty.

TIP

Be generous. Remember colleagues' birthdays, contribute to office collections without complaint and buy your team a drink, an ice cream or surprise sweets now and then. Good bosses are usually generous people and people who are personally mean don't make good managers. When it comes to company cash though, the meaner the better!

Useful Web site: simple yoga stretches you can do at your desk on a bad day from **www.will-harris. com/yoga**.

6

WHEN SETBACKS STRIKE

No matter how careful and conscientious you are, mistakes happen. The man or woman who hasn't made a mistake hasn't made anything. Be prepared to own up to your mistakes. To err is human; to deny responsibility for mistakes is foolish. People who think they're infallible are menaces, no matter how talented they might be. Rigid, blinkered attitudes are not assets in today's workplace; they're liabilities. Bosses tend not to promote people who aren't big enough to own up gracefully. If an error of yours is uncovered, accept responsibility. Say something like:

> 'I'm sorry I miscalculated the figures. It was my mistake, but I can produce a new report if I work late tonight and tomorrow, so I'll do that.'

> 'I managed to lose the report summary, or most of it – my fault not the computer's. I've still got the notes so I'll redo it all this evening.'

Never blame anyone else.

TIP

Never ask if you should redo faulty work. Always take it for granted that you will correct it.

When requests are refused

If your request for something such as a new project, extra resources or training is turned down, accept it philosophically. Keep coming up with new ideas even if some are rejected. A good strategy is to send a brief note, perhaps by e-mail, within 24 hours of a rejection along the lines of: 'Thanks for looking at my idea. I can see it does need more work on it. I'll take up your suggestions and get back to you with fresh ideas – thanks again. David.' In your note, refer to a comment made in the rejection so that it's clear you understand your boss's point of view.

An idea that isn't taken up will not do your career any harm – quite the opposite. The vast majority of employees never offer a single idea for improving their own company. So workers who are 'alive' in this way are very much valued. Keep those ideas coming!

Difficult situations

If the company has to make staff cuts, share the increased workload willingly. There's always a drop in morale after redundancies. Try to keep people's spirits up rather than joining in with the general gloominess. If it was your boss who had to tell people they were being made redundant, he or she has faced a grim task. If you quietly acknowledge this, your comment will go down well.

TIP

When you plan projects build in some setback time to allow for the unexpected. If you don't have to use it, you'll get your project in ahead of time. If you do have to use it, you'll still be on time.

Stay on track

Stamina is probably the number one strength in your promotion kitbag. You need to be able to focus on promotion and tackle your job well, day in, day out. That means you may need to re-energize yourself at work from time to time. Everyone has those headachy 'can't go on' afternoons now and then. Recognize the feeling?

You can beat a bad hour if you:

- tidy something – a drawer, your desktop, a display unit;
- add new names and contacts to a database;
- buy sweets or nuts to share round;
- e-mail a 'positive' friend for a one-line chat.

This is your worst-case scenario: you thought promotion was just round the corner, but someone else gets it this

---

TIP

One way to perk up a more prolonged 'doldrums' time is by buying something new to wear at work. This need not be a major purchase, it could be some budget jewellery, a new shirt, a tie, winter gloves and scarf, or new cologne. You'll freshen up your self-image and give yourself more vitality.

---

time. This is a real setback. Keep smiling! Congratulate the lucky man or woman. Send them a nice note or e-mail. Save your four-letter words for when you get home. Then keep working through your promotion plan as before. Most likely you were just a bit premature – you need to work on getting promoted for a bit longer. Above all, don't get resentful or grumpy. The next promotion could be yours.

TIP

If you're going through a bad time, take up a comforting project to look forward to after work. This could be anything from a small home improvement to cooking a special meal or doing a short easy course.

Are you in 'downtime' this minute? You need superquick fixes if you're to get back on the promotion track! Today you could:

- buy yourself a new paperback by your favourite author, or an inspiring how-to book (try anything by personal power guru Anthony Robbins or mind, body and spirit visionary Leslie Kenton);
- treat yourself to two new magazines on a topic that will please you;
- book up an aromatherapy session soon. Rose geranium is a good oil for stress and depression.
- arrange to play badminton, go paintballing or horse-riding – something you're good at or have always wanted to try.

Think 'strong'

One of the least helpful things to do in a down phase is to get together with a workmate who's also fed-up. You end up having a moaning session and maybe making plans to leave (which could scupper your promotion strategy).

Another unhelpful thing is to go home in the evening and sit staring at the wall. You need to fill your mind with something other than your depression, such as a book, a film, a meal, and perhaps a glass of wine!

Never tell your boss you feel hard done by, or complain that you've been treated unfairly. He or she will just remind you that life isn't fair.

TIP

It's OK to feel down at work. Everyone does. But try not to talk about it. Pretend you're an actor playing a happy worker – smile and chat. Oddly, this seems to work and before long you'll feel better.

Barriers to promotion can come from you. By thinking in a negative way you sabotage your own efforts. Instead of thinking 'This is awful. I can't stand it. I'll never be promoted now' think 'I feel a bit down today. But I've been feeling good here, and I expect to feel good again soon. I expect to be promoted.' (Think 'strong').

Useful Web site for staying calm at work during setbacks: **www.calmcentre.com**

7

TAKE RESPONSIBILITY

Don't just accept responsibility, grasp it. Be the one to deal with a problem, even if it's not a problem that comes strictly within your remit. You can be the one to sort out even small problems, like the cleaning lady not being able to find the bin bags, or a colleague having left her pass-key at home. Get a reputation for being helpful.

A college leaver who joined a contract publishing company as a receptionist often stayed late just to watch the magazines being completed. Since most procedures were done on desktop, she began to pick up the editorial and production stages. She also sussed out which tasks the editorial staff found a nuisance – phone calls chasing copy, fact-checking calls, sending out voucher magazines, faxing text – and she offered to take on some of these, dealing with them when reception was quiet.

Just by observing and copying the editors, she was able to learn a lot – but that alone wouldn't have been enough for promotion. She also chose to shoulder more responsibility. Within a year she had been promoted to editorial assistant, and within three years she was a deputy editor. Five ways to layer **more responsibility** into your job:

● add **more detail** when writing reports – go a bit further;

● **forward plan** your tasks for three months ahead, in writing;

● **coach** a colleague who's finding a system difficult;

● offer to be a **mentor** (if you have experience in company systems and are more mature, you can advise and steer someone younger in their career);

● understand how to manage a **budget.**

Now here are things it's *not* worth taking responsibility for if you want to be promoted. That's not to say these aren't worthwhile but they won't help you to a better job. They might use up your energy on trivia. They are:

● the office noticeboard;

● the first-aid box;

● the stationery cupboard.

Problem-solving

Taking responsibility for solving problems is a key part of being a manager. Observe how managers you admire do it, and learn to copy them. They may tackle an obstacle with:

● a **sense of humour** – making people laugh so they forget their grievances;

● a **non-judgemental attitude** – dealing with the problem without assigning blame;

● a **positive** approach – not wallowing in problems but moving swiftly to solutions.

44

Basically, the excellent manager is a problem-solver and a team player, who acknowledges everyone and treats everyone in the same fair and courteous manner. Such managers show a responsible attitude to others' welfare.

Communicate with more people

Good managers don't hide away in their offices, they're 'visible'. If you're not a natural extrovert, you'll have to make an effort to be more visible. The more you do it, the easier it gets! Try being on cheerful 'having a word' terms with everyone in the office, from receptionist to office cleaner, rather than just chatting to your immediate team. Yes, it does need effort – it's so much easier to come in, sit down and chat only to your team, but that's how most of us can get into a rut.

You'll probably have to go out of your way to have a word with newcomers and people you don't work directly with, but it's worth it. 'How are you?' or 'How's it going?' said with a smile is enough to start you off. Get into the habit of having this brief word with most people, so you get to know more or less everyone in your department or building.

TIP

Listen when people tell you things: try not to 'top' their awful experience with one of yours.

Be a good host

If you're at a work meeting, lunch or reception and feeling slightly exposed, take on a little responsibility (and feel more comfortable at the same time) by:

- offering others food and drinks – playing 'host' rather than guest;
- looking out for company newcomers, and chatting to them;
- showing visitors around;
- offering to do any chauffeuring needed;
- giving out company material, or getting people to sign in;
- volunteering to research something;
- offering to co-ordinate a small committee or project;
- if your guests are from out-of-town, suggesting local beauty spots, sites of historic interest or restaurants they could visit.

When you have a definite role to play, you feel much less reticent. So expanding the scope of what you do will actually increase your confidence. Plus, your helpful attitude can't but be noticed and approved – unlike the rest of the staff you haven't just headed for the drinks tray and chatted to your mates!

What not to do

Warning: taking on more responsibility doesn't mean being bossy, or giving the impression you know better. No matter how brilliant show-offs are at their jobs, employers are wary of them. It's essential that others find you easy and pleasant to work with. Being quietly calm and steady (but not timid) isn't a handicap to promotion.

Seven ways to *dent* career chances:

- boast about how good you are at something;
- try to do too much, too fast, too stressfully;

- criticize the way other people do things;
- make fun of anyone – be very discreet instead;
- gossip – if you don't join in you'll gain respect;
- lose your temper;
- display prejudice – against people who are old, over-weight, gay, from a different culture and so on.

Read it up

It's useful for managers-to-be to have a basic working knowledge of the following three things:

- company law – especially aspects of employment law like hiring and firing, disciplinary procedures, statutory benefits;
- unions and how they work;
- your own company history – ask your HR department for any leaflets.

(You can buy inexpensive how-to books on all aspects of business: try the **Amazon** on-line store for a huge range).

Begin to read a quality newspaper every day – a different one each day if you like. Watch TV documentaries about top business gurus or business advisors giving information to flagging businesses. These programmes are entertaining and easy to watch and through them you'll pick up good nuggets of sound business advice. The more informed you are the better your career prospects.

Useful Web site for books on business, creativity and motivation from *Creativity Unleashed* at **www.cul.co.uk/ books**

CHALLENGE FOR SUCCESS

Challenge embedded notions at work. If something's been done in a certain way for 50 years but doesn't seem to be working well now, try to think of a better way to do it. But remember – don't try to fix things that aren't broken. Bosses like people with common sense who approach change with an open mind.

Someone who tells you firmly 'We've always done it this way and that's the way I'm going to do it' is unlikely to ever be a boss. Yes, there are some traditions worth preserving. One example of this is 'the customer is always right', but ways of dealing with customers have changed. The successful company is changing and evolving all the time. For example, one thing you might challenge is the idea of 'scripted' responses to customers. Ask if you could have a trial run with unscripted responses, and see how many new or repeat orders you can achieve.

Another new trend is encouraging workers to shop on-line from work – making it easier for them to work longer hours. It's essential when offering new ideas either to ask for a trial run, carry one out if you can, or offer some evidence that your idea could work.

Get it right

When you're thinking about ideas or plans for the company, get things right more times than you get them wrong. Don't guess at sales figures or the customer complaints ratio – this sort of information will be available somewhere within the company. HR staff can be your first port of call. They should be able to advise you on where to access factual information. When you're putting ideas in writing, only use hard facts as your background.

Be bold – write proposals or outlines for projects you know you could take on. Don't worry that you'll come over as arrogant or a show-off. Employees who show they want to seize opportunities and can put their ideas in writing delight bosses. If you know you have a good idea, you can almost write your own job description. But remember – don't ask for any money yet! Just outline what you might do, the *benefits* to the company, and the cost (although preferably no cost should be involved).

TIP

Show initiative. Can you think of a way for the company to do something faster? Put it in writing to your boss.

Find mentors

Most people just do their job and go home. But you're career-conscious and you want to get on. You can do your job in a different, more challenging way from your colleagues – maybe by finding a mentor (or being one), trying a bit of networking and deliberately expanding the scope of how you operate.

Can you identify mentors or people who will help you at work? A mentor is a kind of career patron, but in reality this could mean anyone useful and helpful in developing your career. It could be anyone from Tony G in Sales or Mary B in PR to someone in a different company, or in a business club.

The mentors you should consider will have the kind of jobs you aspire to (they'll probably be working at one stage up from you). You'll have met them at a company or industry event and seen they're friendly, approachable and on the same wavelength as you. They will be clearly as keen on work as you are. Don't even try to connect with anyone who seems frosty or very preoccupied – there'll be enough friendly helpful types to approach.

In a large modern company workers are encouraged to share knowledge and be helpful to one another, so e-mail a possible mentor or ask them for 15 minutes of their time. Don't feel shy about this as people love being asked for their advice. Then you can find out the practicalities of the job you're aiming for, such as how they arrange their day, how much time is spent on figures and budgeting, or how many meetings they attend or hold.

Just ask

Ask your mentor about:

● books and magazines they recommend;

- business clubs worth joining;
- useful Web sites;
- when they first got promoted;
- which training courses are most useful;
- the part of their job they find hardest;
- three main qualities important for their role.

Write a few notes afterwards to remind yourself what they've said. Thank your mentor by note or e-mail, and keep in touch for extra advice – they'll enjoy the ego boost of being a sort of career guru!

TIP

Keep your mentoring plans to yourself! Only promotion-hungry workmates are likely to understand. You don't have to justify your career agenda to anyone.

Diversify. Let's say you're a credit controller or a junior systems manager – that doesn't mean you can't learn about sales or marketing or PR. Pick up as much as you can about whatever you're interested in, from business books and contacts within the company. There's nothing to stop you.

Network now

Construct your own network of contacts, and cultivate them. Networking means creating a business friendship, but without the usual slowish friendship development. You can go straight to asking a favour (advice or information on work) from your network contacts. Always send a note or e-mail of thanks promptly. When you meet someone at a seminar or presentation, you'll find you can get to know him or her quite quickly within a day. Follow up that first meeting with a note or e-mail – the person might be friendly enough to suggest a quick coffee, or you could. It's fine for you to make the first move.

At any company event (except the office party when everyone wants to forget work) you can network. You can network at:

- an in-house training session, seminar or conference;
- a conference attended by representatives of many different companies;
- a sales trip or exhibition;
- a reception hosted by your company.

It's essential to have business cards, so create your own from your computer if the company doesn't provide them. Names and e-mails scribbled on napkins and scraps of paper get lost and look scruffy. Hand out your cards generously: once someone has your card and you have his or hers it's very easy to make contact. For some reason, everyone enjoys being given business cards!

TIP

Put warmth into every exchange. Make your dealings with customers, colleagues, managers and network contacts as warm and friendly as possible. Good managers aren't cool and remote. Practise being warm and see how it rewards you.

As you make new career contacts, stay well organized: your contacts may visit you unexpectedly at your office! Make sure you:

- keep a neat desk and briefcase (and perhaps car);
- maintain an up-to-date contacts book;
- ask for business cards or create your own;
- don't have lots of toys, pictures and jokes around your computer.

TIP

Never take your promotion for granted. You have to earn it. And you will!

Useful Web site for being more informed: **www.news-papers.com** which gives a list of online newspapers across the world.

THE JOB'S YOURS!

Take on more and more, steadily and carefully, and wait for the right opportunity to ask for that promotion. It could be when a job vacancy higher up the management ladder is advertised internally, or at your next appraisal meeting.

Applying formally for promotion

Most firms advertise their vacancies internally, so watch the noticeboards and staff newsletters. Monitor the gossip. Word of a resignation or sacking usually gets around before the official memo. Keep an eye on the company's expansion or re-organization plans. There could be an opportunity for you. The more time you have to prepare your application the better.

The job advertisement will ask for written applications. There'll be no exceptions for internal candidates. A word to Joe in Personnel saying you'd like the job won't be good enough. But as a matter of policy companies normally interview internal candidates, so your written application need not be as detailed and comprehensive as if you were writing from the outside. The company will already have most of your CV on file, and they'll know a lot about you. You'll start with a big advantage.

Keep the application brief, but not dismissively so. Set out what you've achieved in your current post, with written evidence to back up your successes, and explain why your promotion would benefit the company. Say you look forward to the opportunity of discussing your application in greater detail should the company want to take it to the interview stage.

Don't assume that because you're an internal candidate the job is yours. There could be other colleagues who are just as promising and as ambitious as you. The company's preference for this post might be for fresh blood from outside.

Be convincing at the interview

Your role at the interview is to convince the interviewer that you can bring new ideas and enthusiasm to the job, plus the valuable detailed knowledge of the company that external candidates won't have. Go well prepared to the interview with a detailed but concise chronicle of your successes. Be confident. Have clear ideas about how you would tackle the new job, especially its problem areas, and some constructive comments about the company's general position and future. Put yourself in the interviewer's shoes, think about the questions you would ask and plan convincing answers. Look for the weaker spots in your own application and be prepared for tough questions on them. When you've done all this, you'll have done your best. All you can do now is wait for the decision.

Handling an appraisal

Approach your appraisal seriously. Remember that the manager doing the appraisal isn't at the head of the corporate food chain. Many managers don't like doing appraisals and are embarrassed by the whole business, especially appraising someone they work closely with every day. If you make it as easy as possible for the appraiser, that's another step up your promotion ladder. Prepare well for your appraisal. This includes going in with practical suggestions for training that would benefit you and the company.

Give credit

When you review your achievements, never claim the credit for other people's good ideas. Not only is this dishonest, but also you'll probably be found out. Not getting due credit is one of the reasons good people leave jobs and go elsewhere, so you could be responsible for this if you take credit for other's work. Instead, give credit where it's due and win brownie points for yourself for getting the best out of people and encouraging initiative. A manager's job is to motivate good people, not push them to the competition next door.

Don't react to criticism

Your appraisal might include some comments from your boss which sound like criticism, but don't spoil your good work by getting cross. Don't react emotionally. If you think the criticism is unfair, say so politely, giving reasons. The employee who is promotion material is not defensive or angry when criticized. You have to accept that not everyone will approve of you and it may be that jealous colleagues do want to push the knife in. Get used to it. Those knives will probably be even sharper when you're promoted!

Asking for more money

When the next pay review comes round, it's time to ask for a salary increase. At this stage be careful not to price yourself out of the market: your increase should reflect your extra work but still make it seem like a company saving. You, one person, are doing the work of another whole or half person but not costing the firm anything like one-and-a-half or two people. Outline in writing the ways in which you've helped the company – particularly in cost-cutting or generating new business – and ask for your salary to be increased, without necessarily putting a figure on it.

Remember:

- never ask for more money saying: 'Jim's doing the same job as me and I want what he earns';

- never ask for more money because you're broke (managing your finances is your responsibility and not the company's);

- gain trust over a period of time by building up a portfolio of successes and achievements;

- even if you've been promoted once, the second promotion isn't automatic.

TIP

Your abilities with the 3 C's – **c**ommunication, **c**oaching and **c**omputer skills – will mark you out for success. Have some achievements to demonstrate each of them. You don't have to be an expert.

Prepare your case

Keep evidence of all you're doing for the company. You need a ring binder or folder in which to keep letters, memos and reports that support your case. Even if a project wasn't a howling success, it could still have added up to useful research. Keep letters or e-mails you get from satisfied customers.

Now is not the time to:

- enquire about sabbaticals – even if you have been with the company a long time;

- ask for an extended holiday, or for leave without pay;

- ask about working in other areas or branches of the company, or abroad.

Consolidate now

This is the time to consolidate all you've done and give more to your current boss. Handling your appraisal and salary review will be the final stages in your first promotion programme – you'll be building on all you've done. You'll already have **demonstrated** what you can do, and provided the **evidence** of success: now you formally **ask** for entry into the next stage up.

Useful Web site to rehearse a job appraisal or a talk: *Authentic Speaking* at **www.speakingcircles.com**.

10

KEEPING AHEAD

Congratulations. Your hard work and the long days have paid off. You've got promotion. But is that the end of the story? You've climbed further up the ladder, but is this where you intend to stay? Is this where the striving stops?

Don't be tempted into complacency. Maintain your hard-earned reputation for hard work and reliability. Promotion doesn't entitle you to late starts and early departures, and it would be unwise to cut corners now. You are shouldering a heavier burden and you've got to show you can cope with it. If necessary, put in more hours.

Another risk is that after a while, when you discover that a manager's situation is far from comfortable, you might think you're 'doing too much' and almost resent the company for the burden it's placing on you. This mood has sabotaged many a promising career. Make sure you remind yourself you wanted both the extra work and the extra benefits.

Get back to your secret promotion plan, but don't exhaust yourself physically or mentally. Take adequate vacations and invest in energy 'fixes' such as regular massage or aromatherapy treatments, health club membership and exercise such as walking and swimming.

Don't be too obvious about making moves for your next promotion. Your boss has sorted you out for the time being: let him or her move on to other things. He or she will want to see you concentrating on your new job. Remember the military maxim: secure your conquered ground before moving on to the next campaign.

Motivate others

To keep on top of the new job, you'll need to build on the leadership skills you've demonstrated already. The ability to inspire others is vital if you're ambitious. You can motivate others by:

● Praising good work – the work doesn't have to be excellent.

● Saying 'thanks'. If you're around when people are leaving the office at the end of the day, don't just say 'goodnight' – say 'thanks'. If you know they've done something well that day, refer to it.

● Not just criticizing when someone is doing something wrong. Instead, explain how it should be done.

● Involving people in projects from the earliest possible moment. Say how you want things done, but invite better, alternative ideas. If there are any, use them and give credit where it's due.

● Trying to get pay increases for good people where you can.

● Leading by example to earn respect.

> ## TIP
>
> Once you're promoted, don't be tempted to 'dump' work on juniors. Delegate carefully: still do the core planning and managing, plus extra tasks. If you begin 'dumping', it will soon be noticed and you may not get the next promotion.

Have a help network

You may be someone who puts in large bursts of work and then gets very tired or even exhausted or depressed. Many managers find this happens. Try to build into your life some 'preventive medicine' for this. Try booking regular holidays and breaks in your diary instead of waiting until you're worn out, then finding that everything's booked up or you can't go because other key staff are away too.

If you're a working mum or single dad, you shouldn't be doing a second shift at home: some cash spent on a cleaner, for example, will take some of the chores away.

Get things delivered

There are shopping delivery services in most cities. Even if you don't feel you need a cleaner, you might welcome an ironing service. See home delivery services, ironing services and the rest as your help network. You should certainly have a list of all your local take-always pinned up in your kitchen. You could buy 'awkward items' like towels and sheets mail order. (The White Company simplifies colour co-ordination! orders@thewhitecompany.co.uk) Try all the home shopping catalogues for electrical and kitchen goods. Don't forget you can use the Internet for shopping. The more you can have delivered, the more of your time is your own.

You may even be able to spend a couple of hours on work when the rest of the weekend runs smoothly, maybe by getting up early on a Sunday morning. The more organized your life is, work done at home will seem less like a chore.

Look after yourself

TIP

Staying fit is essential. The higher up you go at work, the more stress there is. Keeping fit is vital. If you really dislike sports, try to walk for an hour a day on Saturday and Sunday – city walking is fine.

It may be very expensive to belong to a local health club and you may not use it enough to justify the cost. Instead, think in terms of the 'day ticket' including use of all facilities at a spa or leisure hotel. Some hotels do a six or ten visit ticket at a cheap rate.

Keep on top

Don't forget that your very strengths can pull you down – people can ruin their success just by becoming too tired.

TIP

When you're promoted, besides the feeling of success there's also a 'pain barrier' – things just don't feel so comfortable as before. Get through the initial discomfort. You will grow into the new role. Don't even think of jacking it in and demoting yourself.

Then it's tempting just to do the 'easy' things you know you can do well rather than tackle more challenging roles.

There's no point in spoiling your success by putting your head down and becoming too hands-on again. Your bosses want you to organize others and originate ideas, not just be a 'worker bee'. Bigger and more significant ideas will be expected from you as you climb higher up the career ladder. Your salary is your company's investment in you. When you feel worn out, try to take a short break, return to work renewed and put more into your new role. Do not – repeat not – return to your old role, the one you had before you were promoted. This is a trap that many people fall into.

As you move on up, there may be benefits in addition to the cash: private health insurance, share options, profit share, your own team, a company car or your own office. But the demands on your skills, talents and time are greater. Stick to all the principles that secured you your first promotion.

> Useful Web site: still haven't booked that much needed holiday? Try **www.lastminute.com** for in-the-nick-of-time cheap flights and breaks.

Summary

The more responsible and highly paid the job, the fewer applicants there are – two examples of organizations affected by this are the Army and publishing companies. Both these employers attract many candidates at the lower end of the scale, but few candidates for the highly paid demanding positions. Most employers have trouble finding enough staff of the right calibre for the more important roles. Many employees fear taking on too much responsibility.

Visit Kogan Page on-line

Comprehensive information on
Kogan Page titles

Features include

- complete catalogue listings,
  including book reviews and
  descriptions

- on-line discounts on a variety
  of titles

- special monthly promotions

- information and discounts on
  NEW titles and BESTSELLING titles

- a secure shopping basket facility
  for on-line ordering

- infoZones, with links and
  information on specific areas of
  interest

PLUS everything you need to know
about KOGAN PAGE

http://www.kogan-page.co.uk

30 Minutes
... To Improve Your
Networking Skills

HILTON CATT and
PATRICIA SCUDAMORE

KOGAN PAGE

First published in the UK by Kogan Page, 2000

Kogan Page Limited
120 Pentonville Road
London N1 9JN

British Library Cataloguing in Publication Data
A CIP record for this book is available from the British Library.

ISBN 0 7494 3316 7

Typeset by Florence Production Ltd, Stoodleigh, Devon
Printed and bound in Great Britain by Clays Ltd, St Ives plc

The 30 Minutes Series

Titles available are: *30 Minutes* . . .

Before a Meeting

Before a Presentation

Before Your Job Appraisal

Before Your Job Interview

To Boost Your Communication
Skills

To Boost Your Self-Esteem

To Brainstorm Great Ideas

To Deal with Difficult People

To Get Your Own Way

To Get Yourself Promoted

To Improve Telesales
Techniques

To Make the Right Decision

To Make the Right Impression

To Make Yourself Richer

To Manage Information
Overload

To Manage Your Time Better

To Market Yourself

To Master the Internet

To Motivate Your Staff

To Negotiate a Better Deal

To Plan a Project

To Prepare a Job Application

To Solve That Problem

To Succeed in Business
Writing

To Understand the Financial
Pages

To Write a Business Plan

To Write a Marketing Plan

To Write a Report

To Write Sales Letters

Available from all good booksellers.
For further information on the series, please contact:

Kogan Page, 120 Pentonville Road, London N1 9JN
Tel: 020 7278 0433 Fax: 020 7837 6348

www.kogan-page.co.uk

CONTENTS

1

PICKING THE RIGHT PEOPLE TO NETWORK WITH

Networking starts with people you know. But this isn't to say you network with everyone you know. Indeed, from a networking point of view, you need to be very careful about who you include in your circle and, as we shall see shortly, some people are best left well alone.

In setting off on this crash course in improving your networking skills, the first subject we want to look at is how to go about getting onto networking terms with the right people and, conversely, how to make sure you give the wrong people a wide berth.

PROFESSIONAL NETWORKING

This is by way of a definition before we start. The context in which we are using the term networking is that of your work. More properly, we should be referring to such networking as *professional networking* to distinguish it from the kind of networking you do with your family and friends or with those with whom you share your leisure pursuits. Different rules apply to professional networking and you should always make the distinction.

YOUR GREAT NETWORKING SUPERHIGHWAY

A useful way to consider the links in a networking relationship is to compare them to a great superhighway where the traffic is going in both directions. You network someone and they network you back. Someone does you a good turn by effecting an important introduction for you and, a few months later, they want you to do the same for them. This mutually beneficial arrangement of you scratching their back while they scratch yours is what networking is all about and it's fine of course so long as you have no misgivings about the other person. You are happy to put in a good word for them to help them get business. You have no qualms about sharing sensitive information with them. You are prepared to put your reputation on the line by recommending them for a top job.

But what if this isn't the case? What if you have doubts about John or Jenny Doe's work ethics or their personal integrity? Should you be sticking your neck out for them quite so readily?

The answer, needless to say, is no and to illustrate why let's ask Neil to tell us what happened when he found himself on the receiving end of a cry for help from his old friend Harriet.

Neil: Harriet and I go back a long way. We graduated together and we've kept in touch ever since – meeting for a drink or a game of tennis from time to time. About a month ago I received a phone call from Harriet to say she'd lost her job with the firm of management consultants where she'd been working. She blamed it on cutbacks but I had my suspicions. Harriet may be great fun but she will never win any prizes for reliability or organizing herself.

What Harriet wanted me to do, however, was to have a word with Mike, my boss, to see if he could find a slot for her with the firm. A few warning bells immediately sounded off in my head but I couldn't see any way of saying no to Harriet. After all, she'd done so many good turns for me in the past.

The upshot was that Mike offered Harriet a job. Then, on the morning she was supposed to start, she didn't turn up. Mike went ballistic – not surprisingly. He called me into the office and told me not to bother introducing any of my friends ever again, and he's been frosty with me since. As to Harriet, she'd been offered a job somewhere else on better pay. Didn't she think to let Mike know? Unfortunately not, but sadly that's Harriet all over.

NETWORKING WITH PEOPLE WHO COULD LET YOU DOWN

Neil found out the hard way that networking with people who are unsatisfactory for one reason or another usually ends in tears. But while he's contemplating how to get his relationship with Mike back on track perhaps he should be reflecting on how much worse things could have been for him if Harriet had actually joined the firm.

So what's the lesson here? Simply this – never network with anyone who could let you down because they will call in the favours from time to time and you will find it hard to refuse them. Like Neil, the result could be that your reputation suffers in quarters where it matters.

PROPRIETORSHIP OF YOUR NETWORK

Think of your network as a small business over which you have sole proprietorship rights. With your ownership comes responsibility, of course, and not least, the responsibility for hire and fire. In exercising this responsibility:

- **Be firm**. Strike anyone off your network who doesn't measure up.

- **Don't fudge**. As far as membership of your network is concerned, never be tempted to give anyone the benefit of the doubt. Don't give second chances to those who let you down. View one bad experience as enough.

- **Be flexible**. Allow for the fact that people change and sometimes for the worse. Remember that, as far as your network is concerned, there's no such thing as life membership.

PROACTIVE AND REACTIVE NETWORKING

At this juncture, let's introduce you to some terminology.

Proactive networking is the networking you instigate. If you like, it is the outbound traffic on your great networking superhighway. Proactive networking will be generated by some need you have – a need, say, for an introduction or for someone to put in a good word for you or because you need access to some information.

Reactive networking, conversely, is the networking that comes the other way (the inbound traffic). It is generated by the needs of others, needs they will see you as being able to satisfy.

Proactive and reactive networking are interdependent. One thrives on the other and this bouncing backwards and forwards of messages is the key to understanding what makes networks work.

SEVERING YOUR NETWORKING LINKS WITH PEOPLE WHO DON'T MEASURE UP

How do you do this?

If you want to close off one of your superhighways, the first step to take is to stop using it. Don't send any more traffic off down the outbound lane and you'll find the traffic coming back the other way has a natural tendency to dry up. Why? Networks need to be constantly switching from the proactive to the reactive and back again in order to thrive and without this constant switching they soon wither and die. Networking with someone effectively gives them an open invitation to network you back, but without this open invitation they will be less sure of their ground and think twice before picking up the phone. A few polite but firm cold shoulders should serve to put the final kiss of

---

TIP

Don't network with people who are awkward or who won't help. Put them on the list for de-selection straight away.

---

death on any networking relationships you no longer wish to continue with. Later in the book you'll be learning about approachability and availability. If you want to freeze someone out these are lessons you need to apply in reverse.

TAKING STOCK OF YOUR NETWORK

Having pruned out the dead wood from your network along with any parasites, it's time to cast your eyes over what's left.

Sadly, the term 'networking' is a complete turn-off for many people largely because it conjures up images of endless rounds of gossipy social gatherings of the sort they dread. First point first therefore: everyone in a career has got a professional network, whether they would choose the term or not. It could almost be described as unavoidable.

Who features on the typical professional network? A snapshot usually reveals a complete mix of people such as:

- work colleagues past and present, including bosses, peers and subordinates;

- other business contacts such as customers and suppliers;

- people you meet through going on external courses or because you belong to a professional body.

Networks also reflect the routes that careers have followed. For example, someone who has moved around a lot or worked overseas will have a very different network to someone whose experience is essentially one company.

SIZE – AND WHETHER IT MATTERS

A lot of the effort that goes into professional networks is directed at making them grow bigger. The more people you can make friends with and influence, the better it is for you – or so we are told. But is this necessarily true? The answer is 'not always' – for the following reasons:

- The bigger a network gets, the harder it is to control. Controlling networks (making them do what you want them to do) is a vital part of good networking practice – a subject we will be looking at later. A network that is out of control is dangerous and can turn round and deal you lethal blows.

- The dash for growth can sometimes lead to a relaxation of the selection standards – meaning you admit people who shouldn't really be there.

TIP

One way to grow your network is by putting some external dimensions onto it, ie seek to network with people other than your work colleagues (something you will find beneficial when, for example, you want to use networking to access jobs for you or as a source of information on conditions outside your own company). How do you do this? Join your appropriate professional body and go along to the meetings. Go on external courses. Attend conferences. See if there are any working parties or special interest groups you could join. Accept that this will mean giving up some of your own time.

- It adds to the (false) impression that networking is the preserve of social climbers and extrovert personality types. This can lead to a whole section of people feeling excluded.

Networks are best viewed as organic and not in need of any artificial growth stimulants. So, to a large extent, let the size of your network take care of itself. If you want to put more effort in anywhere, put it into making your existing network work for you and deliver the outcomes you are seeking to achieve.

GROWING NETWORKS AGAINST TARGETED CAREER AIMS

Whilst deprecating growth for growth's sake and trying to network with an ever-increasing number of people with no precise aim, we take quite a different view of getting onto networking terms with people who can influence career outcomes for you.

In our book *The Power of Networking* (also published by Kogan Page) we tell the story of the young apprentice who discovered his remote and rather ill-dispositioned managing director was addicted to the game of golf. With his eye to the main chance, the apprentice immediately bought himself a set of clubs and started taking lessons. Once proficient, the plan was to invite the managing director for a round one Saturday morning.

We never did hear how our apprentice got on but his story illustrates how there is a right and a wrong way of going about striking up a networking relationship with someone. Get it wrong and you could be putting yourself out of favour to the extent where the recipient of your networking overtures is frantically trying to work out how best to keep you at an arm's length. All the worse for you, of course, if the person concerned is someone whose influence could have a profound effect on the direction of your career.

THE BOND OF COMMON INTEREST AND SHARED EXPERIENCE

What any effective network has to have is a thread of common interest and/or shared experience – a bonding agent that will hold it together. In a family, for instance, the common interest is provided by the home, the family's economic well-being, the care of children and dependants, and so on. The shared experience, on the other hand, is to be found in family life: the high spots and the low spots, the coming through hardship together, the sharing of joy and sorrow.

With a professional network, the thread of common interest and/or shared experience is to be found in the work you do. Common interest, for example, will figure in the objectives of the organization to which you belong. If it is a commercial organization, maximizing the profit figure or seeing off competition will be items of common interest. As for shared experience, this could be pulling through a bad patch together or bringing a new product on stream.

The point to take in here is that there should be no need to invent pretexts for professional networking. The pretext is already there in the shape of your work. So what our young apprentice was seeking to do (have a networking relationship with the managing director based on the game of golf) was not really necessary. If his networking stood any chance of getting off the ground at all, the best basis for it was his and the managing director's shared experience of working together for the same organization.

PICKING THE RIGHT PEOPLE TO NETWORK WITH

In deciding who to bring into your networking circle you need first of all to define what you are seeking to achieve from your networking, ie your aims.

Aims vary enormously from one person to the next. For example, your aim could be trying to get a seat on the board of your company. Alternatively, it could be looking to make a complete change in the direction of your career. If you are thinking of going freelance, it could be seeking to get enough capital together to see you through your start-up period. With all of these aims there is usually someone somewhere who can influence the outcomes for you. This is not just the decision-makers themselves but people who have the ear of the decision-makers or people who are adept at pulling strings and moving behind the scenes.

GETTING THE NETWORK GOING

Having identified who you want to get onto networking terms with, the next question is how to get the ball rolling. At this point let's introduce Dean. Dean is going to tell you about how he started networking with someone who proved to be very useful to him:

Dean: I've been trying to get a posting to our Hong Kong office for almost two years and I have discussed this with my boss, Anna, on numerous occasions. Anna, for her part, simply seems to procrastinate and my worst fear is that she is doing this on purpose. The reason? My skills would be hard to replace and I wouldn't put it past Anna to put her own interests first. To add to my frustration, there have been several vacancies in the Hong Kong office recently and they have all been filled by outsiders.

I considered going over Anna's head and having a word with Gavin, the senior partner. This, I realized straight away, would be a high-risk game. One, Anna wouldn't like it and, two, Gavin being Gavin would be hesitant about doing anything that would undermine her.

OK, so it looks like Dean has fallen into the trap of being too useful (he wouldn't be the first!). But can networking help him? Let's find out:

Dean: Quite by chance I bumped into Florence on a trip to the vending machine. Like me, Florence started on the graduate training programme and she now works as a PA in the partners' office. We got talking and I told her about the problems I was having. She said she was sorry and promised to think of ways in which she could help.

Now let Florence take over the story:

Florence: I like Dean. He is a very positive person who is always prepared to give anyone a helping hand. In my own case, we had a panic in the office a few months back. Typical of Dean, he offered to stay behind and did the running up and down to the photo-copier while I put the finishing touches to a huge report for a client that had to be ready for the couriers by 7 pm. As to Anna, good at her job she may be, but I could well believe her capable of putting obstacles in Dean's path.

I was sad to see Dean so down in the dumps and I rang him that same evening to say that I thought we ought to make Gavin aware of what was going on. At first Dean seemed reluctant. Guessing the reason, I told him I would make sure Gavin understood his concerns about going behind Anna's back.

Over to Gavin for the upshot:

Gavin: I was quite surprised to hear what Florence had to tell me about Dean. I had no idea he wanted to work in Hong Kong, though I could see straight away what a great asset he would be to the team in the Far East. What concerned me most though was that he should feel his career path was being blocked. We need committed young people like Dean and it would be a tragedy if he decided to leave. I was therefore very grateful to Florence for putting the word in my ear. We've got a retirement in Hong Kong coming up shortly, so what I'll do is go to Anna and tell her I think Dean is exactly the right person for the job. She'll gripe of course about having her staff taken off her, which will give me an opportunity to give her a lecture about never standing in the way of bright young people who want to get on.

Proof perhaps that to get where you want to get in life you occasionally have to pull a few strings. Not that Dean instigated this. The suggestion to pull strings came from Florence.

Key points to pick out from this case study are as follows:

- Quite unintentionally, Dean got himself onto networking terms with Florence by being helpful to her.

- The help was unsolicited.

- Because of her job Florence had the ear of the partners. She is therefore a good person to be on networking terms with.

> **TIP**
>
> If you want to strike up a networking relationship with someone, start by doing them a good turn. Little acts of help and kindness come few and far between in today's hustle-bustle world, so your gesture certainly won't go unnoticed. What you will be doing though is putting some inbound (reactive) traffic on your super-highway which will prepare the ground for when you want to send out the signals the other way.

One last, but very important point: the networking between Dean and Florence only worked because Dean projected a good image and it is interesting to speculate on what would have happened if this had not been the case. Would Florence have been quite so keen to take up his case with Gavin? Would she have stuck her neck out for him? Image and its importance in networking is what we will be looking at in the next chapter.

REVIEWING THE PERFORMANCE OF NEW MEMBERS OF YOUR NETWORK

As part of your good management of your network, put any new recruits on a trial period before you confer full membership rights on them. See how they perform the first few times you have occasion to network with them. Stand by to take action if you should find they don't come up to scratch.

ACTION NOTEPAD

- Identify any people you're networking with who could let you down. Take steps to remove them.

- Manage your network. Remember, as far as your network is concerned, it's you who's in charge (no one else).

- Don't put all your efforts into trying to network with more and more people. Give the time instead to making better use of your existing contacts (the benefits will be more immediate).

- Think through your aims. Identify any people who could help you achieve those aims.

- Find ways of getting onto networking terms with people who are in a position to pull strings for you. Help them if they need help. Feed them information where information would be useful to them.

2

PROJECTING THE RIGHT IMAGE

Why should anyone want to network with you? We ask this question not to fill you with self-doubt and paranoia but to get you to focus on the very real issue of image. How do you come across to people you know and how does the image you project affect your ability to network with them?

THE LIFELONG INTERVIEW

Imagine you've applied for a top job with a leading company and you're going along for your first interview. You'll be taking great pains over your appearance, of course. You'll probably rehearse a few good answers to the questions you're likely to be asked. You'll psych yourself up for the occasion and, when you're actually sitting in the hot seat, you'll be very careful not to say anything that could put you in a bad light. Indeed, if there are any grey areas in your track record, you'll be doing your best to draw a veil over them.

Not so though with people you come into contact with in the daily course of your work. You are less mindful of the image you project and, on occasions, you may even let a glimpse of one of the less endearing parts of your character slip out (we've all got a few of those!). Needless to say, the problem here is that we are talking about projecting an image day in day out rather than over the 45–60 minutes that's the norm for most job interviews. Harder? Of course it is and this is what we mean by the *lifelong interview*. It calls for a level of consistency and application that's not easy to achieve. It means for instance:

- You don't have off days.
- You have to be 100% reliable – you get back to people when you say you will.
- You complete your work to targets.
- Your appearance is always up to scratch (don't be the first to dress down!).
- You refrain from running down your colleagues and bosses behind their backs (keep your opinions to yourself).
- You don't whinge and whine (don't use your colleagues as sounding boards whenever you feel you're being given a hard time).
- You put the gloss you normally save up for job interviews into every day.

KEEPING YOUR FLAWS TO YOURSELF

One of the more difficult aspects of the lifelong interview to put into practice is learning to keep your flaws to yourself – difficult, because there's a natural tendency to form close relationships with people you meet through your work. Here's an example:

Tania: The CEO called me into his office the other day and asked me if I knew anyone with the right experience to head up the new materials-handling division. My thoughts turned immediately to Graeme. Graeme and I worked together in my previous company and we know one another well. Graeme has exactly the right experience and, what's more, I happen to know he's not very happy with his job at the moment and anxious to make a move. Why did I hesitate about mentioning his name? Graeme had an alcohol problem about 10 years ago – something he told me in confidence. The problem, it seems, was brought on by pressure of work and resulted in him losing a senior management position with one of the market leaders in the industry. Getting the new division up and running isn't going to be any pushover, that's for certain, hence it bothered me that, put under pressure again, Graeme would go back on the bottle. I thought about it carefully and, after much soul-searching, I told the CEO that I couldn't think of anyone suitable.

Tania played safe and who can blame her? With anyone she recommends she will be putting her own reputation on the line, so giving Graeme a miss makes a lot of sense.

What's clear from this case study is that confiding to Tania cost Graeme the opportunity of a job (a job it sounds like he needed) and this illustrates how, contrary to popular belief, getting too close to someone in a professional networking relationship can be a mistake. The odd indiscretion or insight into some darker side of your personality

---

TIP

'It's who you know' used to be the catchphrase to describe how you got on in life. Today it's truer to say 'It's who you know and what they know about you'.

---

can slip out and, as in Graeme's case, the penalty will be in years to come. Exactly the same goes for letting your hair down in front of colleagues. What you did at the office party often comes back to haunt you.

The lesson? Always keep a careful control on the messages you feed out. In particular, beware of unintentionally using your network to disseminate damaging information (damaging to you, that is). Note: control is a key networking word and we shall be coming back to it time and time again.

ENSURING YOUR APPROACHABILITY

People have got to feel they are going to gain something from networking with you – emphasizing the importance of being receptive to the approaches that come zooming in on the inbound lane of your great superhighway. Being helpful and welcoming is therefore an important part of your image and one you need to cultivate. Conversely what you must never do is put the shutters up to anyone who networks with you either because you're too busy or because what they're asking you to do seems like a tall order. Instead always have the time of day for them. Always give them the impression that being on your network confers special privileges. In short, nothing should ever seem like too much trouble.

Easy? It should be, but to see how things can go wrong let's look at how Ali dealt with a call for help from Ruth.

Ali: She rang at about 8 o'clock one evening just as I was sitting down to eat a meal. She was putting the finishing touches to her CV and wanted to run it past me before sending it off in the post. Couldn't it wait? Ruth said no – the deadline for posting applications for the job she was interested in was the very next day. She wanted to fax it to me straight away.

Much as I like Ruth, I felt annoyed with her. She'd obviously left her CV till the last minute and I'd had a long, hard day. I ended up therefore telling her I couldn't help. I made the excuse I was meeting someone in town and was just on my way out when she rang.

The problem for Ali will be the next time she wants a favour from Ruth. When she does, she shouldn't be too surprised if she finds she gets a return dose of the cold shoulder treatment.

Lessons to be learned here are:

- Approachability frequently comes into conflict with the busy lives we all lead.
- Lack of approachability puts the kiss of death on networking. It kills off the traffic on the inbound lane.
- Being short or less helpful than we can be because one of our network contacts happens to catch us at a bad moment transmits an immediate signal which the person at the other end will be quick to pick up (be careful therefore about those long, drawn-out sighs!).

A point in passing here is that if the aim is to lose someone from your network (eg someone you no longer trust), then reversing your approachability and putting up the shutters should have the desired effect.

ACTION NOTEPAD

- Put on the gloss every day. Don't save your best image for interviews and special occasions.

- Control the messages you feed out about yourself. Don't use your networks to broadcast your flaws.

- Always have the time of day for your contacts. Give special priority to dealing with their needs.

- Do your best for your contacts. Let them see you are worth networking with.

3

GETTING THE INFRASTRUCTURE IN PLACE

As with any business, your network needs the right infrastructure to enable it to function properly, and in this chapter we will be looking at the kind of things you need to consider and, when you've got them, how to put them to best use.

AVAILABILITY

First, let's look at availability. Availability is about providing the wherewithal for your contacts to be able to reach you. Availability goes hand in hand with approachability – the subject we looked at in the last chapter. Approachability and availability are what keeps the traffic on the inbound lane of your great superhighway moving and what this means is that you must make sure you're not putting any obstacles in the paths of people who want to network with you. On the contrary, you need to be doing all in your powers to make it easy for them. The penalty for getting this wrong? You acquire the reputation of being one of those nightmare people who it's impossible to get to speak to. As a consequence, the people who're trying to network with you give up. The traffic on your inbound lane dwindles to a trickle and you're left wondering why.

Keeping your inbound lane clear is important for another reason. Some of the traffic on it will be in response to your *proactive* networking. So, for instance, if you've been putting the word round that you're looking for another job, some of the calls coming in could be from contacts who've come up with something interesting for you. Because of your lack of availability, however, you frustrate their attempts to get through and, as a consequence, you miss out on a chance. You are also making life difficult for them, meaning you score a bad point on your lifelong interview.

Approachability and availability are the twin pillars of good networking practice and you need to work on them. In particular you need to match your availability to your lifestyle and work patterns, and with the vast array of communication technology at your disposal today there is really no excuse for being hard to contact. Is there?

CHECKING OUT YOUR AVAILABILITY

If you're availability is bad, the chances are you'll be the last person to know about it. Here's an example:

Seb: I heard about an exciting business opportunity the other day. It consists of providing a large company with a complete recruitment and training package associated with the opening of one of their new distribution centres. But, whilst my organization has the expertise to do the recruitment, we don't have anyone who can handle operator training in warehouse skills up to acknowledged industry standards. It was here where my thoughts turned to Chas. Chas was the training manager in my last company up to when he was made redundant two months ago. I happen to

---

TIP

People who complain that no-one ever networks with them usually have their lack of availability to blame. So common is this problem that an *availability audit* is something we recommend to anyone aspiring to improve their networking skills. An availability audit means putting yourself in the position of someone trying to get hold of you. How easy would they find it? How would they get on if, for confidentiality reasons, they needed to speak to you at home in the evening? Would you be in? Would anyone be in? How many times would they find the number engaged? The idea of an availability audit is to throw up some points for action, such as, for example:

- Could you benefit from voice mail to take messages on your office phone extension?

- Is it time you got an answering machine at home or installed a second line?

- Do you need to introduce some domestic disciplines (like telling teenagers to spend less time on their calls)?

---

know Chas is looking for a stop-gap to tide him over while he finds another training manager's job – so this is why I thought he would be interested in doing a three-month contract for us. What happened when I tried to contact him at his home? The number rang out and there was no reply. I tried again in the evening only to find the line was permanently engaged. Puzzled, I didn't know what to do next. In the end my boss told me we'd have to forget Chas and find someone else to do the training. It was a pity really. Chas was by far the best man for the job.

Most failings in availability have pretty basic causes. In Chas's case he was spending his days brushing up on his IT skills at the local adult learning centre. In the evenings he was surfing the Internet, thus preventing any incoming calls from getting through. Chas was oblivious to the fact that Seb was trying to get hold of him. To this day he doesn't realize his lack of availability cost him a lucrative contract with Seb's firm (and the handy cash that went with it).

INVESTING IN AVAILABILITY

With the advent of mobile phones, tele-messaging, combined phones, faxes and answering machines, e-mail, features on standard phones such as call diversion and call-waiting signals, phone companies offering one number contactability etc, there is clearly a lot out there for budding networkers to spend their money on.

Will it help you? The answer to this question is it depends a lot on your life patterns. For example, if you work nine to five and spend most evenings at home, you shouldn't present too many challenges to someone wanting to get hold of you. If you work erratic hours, however, or if you travel a lot on business, investment in communications technology is clearly going to enhance your ability to network with people tremendously. Here, working out your own solutions is part of the fun – and remember that availability is something you should always be striving to perfect. Keep your eyes open therefore for 'anything new' on the market. This is a field in which things are changing almost daily.

BROADCASTING YOUR AVAILABILITY

Irrespective of how much you spend on the infrastructure of your professional network, it won't do you a lot of good if no one knows about it. People you network with need to have the following information:

- your home and work addresses and telephone numbers;

- the number of your mobile phone;

- your e-mail address (if you have one);

- any other way of contacting you (eg do you have a fax machine at home? If so, what number do users dial to access it?).

A good place to put all this information is on a personal business card, which you can either produce yourself on your own PC or ask the local print shop to produce for you (either way, it's not going to cost you a lot). Here is an example:

Stephanie Judd
Judd Computer Services, 1 Main Street,
Anytown AT1 X99
Phone: Office: 333 333 333
         Home: 555 555 555
         Mobile: 888 888 888
e-mail: stephaniejudd@xx.co.uk

Having your phone numbers listed and identified as home, office, mobile, etc alongside your e-mail address and/or your private fax number gives your contacts all the information they need in one place if they have to get hold of you in a hurry for any reason. Remember to advise your contacts if your numbers should change, eg because you move jobs. What's the best way to do this? By having a new card printed and sending it out with instructions to destroy the old one. (See also what we've got to say about mailshots a few pages on.)

USING YOUR AVAILABILITY CORRECTLY

How your networking benefits from investment in technology also depends on how disciplined you are in the way you use it.

A common problem here is people who don't check their answering machines. The same goes for people who don't look at their e-mails regularly. Sadly, failing to respond to a contact in an acceptable period of time (worse still, failing to respond at all) sends out an immediate negative message. You don't rate the person as important enough to break into your daily routines – or that's the way it seems. Even if apologies are accepted, the fact you don't check your messaging devices systematically won't do you a lot of good on the lifelong interview front.

What if your lifestyle and/or work patterns make it difficult for you to check faxes and e-mails regularly? Our answer would be don't use them or at least don't advertise their existence as far as your network contacts are concerned.

WHAT TO DO IF YOU FIND NO ONE IS NETWORKING WITH YOU

Go through this short checklist and see if you can put your finger on the problem. Doing this will also act as a fail-safe to make sure you've taken in all that we've covered so far.

- Are you trying to network with people with whom you have no common interest/shared experience? If so, stop and think again.

- Are you spreading your net sufficiently by joining professional bodies and using other opportunities to meet people outside your own firm? If not, start today by identifying three ways in which you could do this. Devise a plan and then decide how your are going to put it into effect.

- How do you measure up as far as projecting the work-perfect and person-perfect image goes? If you suspect your image may be slightly tarnished, start today on getting it right. Your networking will benefit from turning over a new leaf.

- Are you responding correctly to people trying to network with you? Are you being as helpful as you can be? A sign that your approachability is going wrong is when people don't come back.

- Are you getting too close to people you meet through

the course of your work? Are you revealing aspects of your character that you should really be keeping to yourself? If so, learn from your mistakes and make sure in future you control the messages you feed out about yourself.

- Is it difficult to get hold of you? Have you tried doing an availability audit, and if so, what was the result? If availability is your problem, take urgent steps to do something about it.

- Is your availability sufficiently advertised? Are the people you would like to network with aware of how to get hold of you? If not, follow the advice in this chapter.

- Are you rigorous about reading your e-mails regularly and checking the messages on your answering machine? Are you equally rigorous about getting back to people who have left messages?

If you can honestly put a tick alongside each of these bullet points, then you are well on your way to becoming a good networker. Have patience and your effort will pay off.

KEEPING DETAILS OF YOUR NETWORK CONTACTS

Back to infrastructure. If you haven't already got it, something you need is a place to keep details of all your network contacts, including details of how to get hold of them. An address book or a personal organizer immediately springs to mind and this satisfies one important criterion: you need your contact file to be in portable form so you can have it to hand at all times. Portability, however, invites the possibility of loss, so always keep a back-up copy of your contact file, eg a card system that you keep at home or, perhaps better still, a file stored on disk.

MAILSHOTTING
YOUR NETWORK

Why is your contact file better stored on disk? For the simple reason that it facilitates what we want to talk about next.

From time to time you will need to communicate with your contacts, eg to advise them of a new telephone number or if you change jobs. If your IT skills are up to it, the easiest way to do this is by using the mailmerge facility on your PC software to produce a set of personalized letters. As well as communicating the information you need to communicate, these will look good (good for your person-perfect image) and remind everyone in a very visible form that you're still there (the fact that networks occasionally need a little nudge to keep the two-way traffic flowing is a subject we will be touching on in the next chapter).

What about really stepping up a gear and producing an occasional newsletter for your contacts? A bit like a company house journal except the news will be all about you? We must confess to having reservations about newsletters, especially the sort that degenerate into toe-curling yarns about what people get up to at the weekends or what they've been doing with the kids. Our advice? Don't do it unless you've got something to say that's (a) interesting and (b) connected with your work, eg if you've been on a business trip overseas. Remember we're talking about professional networking here.

CREATING SPACE
FOR YOURSELF

Is there anything else you need in the way of infrastructure?

Because of its very nature, a lot of networking is carried on from home. Either it's easier to get hold of contacts in the evening or the subject matter you want to talk about is not for the ears of people in the office. This begs the question: do you have anywhere sufficiently private at home and free from distracting background noises (eg barking dogs or the sound of a television)? If the answer is no, then take steps to create a bit of space for yourself. At the very minimum this means an extension off your phone into a quiet room. Better still is if you use a room at home as an office. Here is where you could install a separate phone/fax/e-mail line with 'hands off' instructions as far as other members of your family are concerned.

VIEW YOUR NETWORKING
AS IMPORTANT

This underlies everything we've had to say about infrastructure. Networks – your cultivation of them and the way you use them – can have a significant bearing on the progress of your career. So don't neglect them by under-resourcing them. Instead give them the proper respect they deserve and you'll find that when you have a need for them, they'll be there, waiting to serve you.

ACTION NOTEPAD

- Pay attention to your approachability and availability. Make sure you are easy to deal with.

- Let people see they've got something to gain from networking with you. Do your best for them. Let them see you as a person who gets results.

- Take stock of your work patterns and domestic routines. Identify where modern communications technology could help improve your availability. Invest accordingly.

- Make sure your contacts know how to get hold of you.

- Make sure your availability works. Make sure you're not the cause of your own problems by failing to check e-mails and message-taking devices regularly and routinely.

4

GETTING YOUR NETWORKS TO PERFORM EFFECTIVELY

'Perform' in this context means perform for **you**.

Having your very own professional network at your disposal is no use to you at all unless it is capable of delivering the outcomes you are seeking to achieve. Here is where the fine-tuning comes in: recognizing the tremendous power of networking and channelling it in directions you want it to go in, or, if you like, taming the beast and making it respond to your instructions.

SMALL WORLDS

There is an inherent problem in networking and it is this. It will only ever access small worlds for you and this, in turn, reflects:

- the number of people who will pass the selection test for your network will never be that many;

- the geographical areas in which you work;

- the profession/trade/line of business in which you are engaged.

Outside these small worlds the power of your networking diminishes significantly. For instance, your professional network will probably not be a lot of help to you if you want to move into a completely different career.

A corollary of these small worlds is that they are often quite tightly knit – meaning there is a lot of potential for information you share with network contacts reaching other ears, including the wrong ones. Here is an example:

> *Marcia:* I put in an application to XYZ Industries, who happen to be one of our biggest competitors. One of my colleagues, Brett, used to work for XYZ Industries so I had a quiet word with him to see if I could get some inside information on the way they operate. Brett was very helpful and gave me lots of useful low-down. But what I didn't bargain for was that Brett would tell Lester that I was thinking of going to work for XYZ and Lester being Lester spilt the beans to Ann, my boss. The result was a very heated discussion in which Ann came very close to telling me to collect my cards (like the rest of our top management team there is no love lost between Ann and XYZ!).

Office tittle-tattle maybe, but, as far as Marcia is concerned, the damage is done – damage in terms of damage to her relationship with her boss, Ann and, through Ann, with the rest of the top brass in her company. What went wrong of course was the failing on Marcia's part to instil into Brett the need for strictest confidence. Crystal-clear instructions should have been given to him not to discuss the matter with anyone else, together with the reason.

KEEPING YOUR NETWORKS UNDER CONTROL

A network that is out of control is a network that won't serve you well and, as in Marcia's case, it is one that could let you down very badly indeed. The lesson? With pro-active networking the messages you feed out to your contacts need to be very precise and defined. Notably they should be **complete** messages, meaning:

- If the subject matter is confidential, they should include instructions not to discuss the matter with anyone except yourself – and the reason why.

- You should define in exact terms what you want your contact to do for you – this is to prevent them doing something else, either because they don't understand where you're coming from or because they think they're helping you (usually they're not!).

- You should set out any time parameters, so if, for example, you need some information by next week, your contact is fully aware of the fact.

- If you want your contact to report back to you at certain points, you should make this absolutely clear – for example, if you're using your contact to access a job opportunity, you may want him or her to find out the salary first, ie before you decide whether to put in an application.

TAPPING INTO OTHER PEOPLE'S NETWORKS

No-one in the world is more than six phone calls away and this tantalizing prospect has served to inspire a whole generation of budding networkers! Sadly, however, the reality is rather different, but before we start pouring too much cold water on claims that you can network with practically anyone, let's take a closer look at what happens when you have dealings with contacts second- and third-hand. More to the point, let's identify the snags, then see what we can do to iron some of them out. In short, let's see what we can do to make extended networking of this kind work for you.

Back to basics first. Everyone has a network – a network that is different to everyone else's. This means that people you network with will have networks that are different to yours. Some of the people will be the same because you have moved in similar circles, but some won't, and, with extended networking in mind, it is this latter group that we need to be focusing on. On closer inspection, however, we find that these contacts of contacts divide into three sub-groups:

- **first**, people you know but who you choose not to network with (for example, people you find unsatisfactory or untrustworthy);

- **second**, people you know and who you have nothing against but who you are not on networking terms with;

- **third**, people you don't know.

The first sub-group we can, of course, put to one side straight away. Now let's look at one of the big problems of networking through intermediaries: the control you need to have over what's going on has to be exercised by others and, needless to say, the further you go down one of these networking chains, the harder the control becomes. As a consequence the kind of dangers we looked at a few pages back start to rear their ugly heads. The wrong ears could pick up the fact you're on the look out for another job. Your aims could be misinterpreted and you could find yourself being steered onto a course you don't want to follow. All sorts of things can happen.

How can you avoid this? One option open to you is to forge a direct link with your contact's contacts, ie bring them onto your network and under your own (better) control. With the second of the three sub-groups (individuals you know and who are acceptable to you) networking direct instead of by proxy is an avenue you could certainly explore.

But what about the last group (the people you don't know). Here you are left with two choices: either you ask your contact to effect an introduction with a view to striking up a direct networking relationship, or you trust your contact to exercise the control for you, ie you delegate the task but with clear terms of reference.

With networking down a chain, however, a dilemma can and often does arise. A further case study will help to illustrate this.

Sam: I saw a job advertised in the newspaper the other day that sounded right up my street. Everything seemed right: the salary, the location, the prospects for further training – the only snag was the company was one I'd never heard of before. Who could I turn to for information? My immediate thought was Amrik. It turned out, however, that Amrik was little the wiser than me, though he said he knew someone who he thought could help. Half an hour later Amrik rang me back. He said he'd spoken to his contact but the feedback wasn't very good. The company had the reputation of being a hire and fire organization with a high turnover of staff and the advice was to steer well clear.

The dilemma for Sam is whether to proceed with his application or not. The problem is he doesn't know Amrik's contact, so he doesn't know how much faith to put in the information he's been given. What should he do next?

Where the subject of the networking could have important consequences for you (as in Sam's case) a sensible step to take is to seek corroboration of any information that has come to you down a chain (irrespective of whether it conforms with what you want to hear or not). You can do this by tapping into more than one source, ie ring round a few more of your contacts.

WARNING!

Networking with people you don't know is potentially dangerous. Don't do it unless you have to. Even then, exert as much control over what's going on as you possibly can.

KNOWING WHEN TO TAKE MATTERS INTO YOUR OWN HANDS

Networking is great at opening doors but there comes a point (always) when it is best for you to start dealing direct. Take networking for a job as an example. A contact may be great at doing the sounding out for you and effecting the introductions, but when it gets to the nitty-gritty like defining the responsibilities or negotiating the pay, this is best done by you. Why? Misunderstanding creeps in, nuances get missed, all sorts of things can happen which could go on to have a bearing on your future.

For this reason it is important to define at the outset what you expect your networking to achieve for you. When that aim has been met, it's time for your contact to step aside and let you take over. Note: part of keeping control is telling your contacts how far you want them to go.

KEEPING THE TWO-WAY TRAFFIC FLOWING

A common experience is to find you have a need for networking then discover your network is no longer there. The name of your contact in ABC Industries has slipped your memory; Jo who worked for DEF & Associates has moved on (no-one can recall where); Tim's number is no longer in the phone book, and you're worried about ringing Charlie simply because it's been such a long time since the two of you last spoke.

What this emphasizes is that networks thrive on use. The more traffic there is whizzing backwards and forwards, the more effectively your network will perform for you or – to put it another way – networking doesn't benefit from the stop–start treatment. It needs to be ongoing.

How do you achieve this? One way we've looked at already – by taking out the obstacles and ensuring that your approachability and availability works at all times. But this doesn't take away the fact that you may not have a need to speak to certain individuals on a very regular basis. What then? The answer is that this is where a bit of cheating comes in. Ring them on an invented pretext. You need a second opinion on something or there could be some interesting information on a mutual acquaintance that you thought to pass on – the subject almost doesn't matter. The fact that you're there on the end of the phone is all that counts. It serves not just as a reminder of your existence but also of your approachability and availability. Any feeling of awkwardness that surrounds relationships with people you haven't spoken to for a long time will automatically be taken away.

Of course, inventing a pretext won't be necessary if you've got some genuine reason for ringing up – like you've moved jobs or your phone number has changed.

TIP

Run through your list of contacts from time to time and ask yourself when you last spoke to them. If 12 months or more have lapsed then take the emergency resuscitation action described above. Failing to do this could mean a link of your network falls into disuse. When you need it, it won't be there.

ACTION NOTEPAD

- Identify what you want your networking to achieve (a clear aim).

- Control the messages you feed out. Make sure they're consistent with the aim.

- Don't use your contacts as a sounding board for your grouses and groans. It communicates no precise aim and there is danger of you being misunderstood.

- Tell your contacts exactly what you expect of them. Don't leave them to make their own interpretations.

- Where confidentiality is of the essence always impress this on your contacts. Explain the reasons.

- Don't delegate to your contacts the jobs you should be doing yourself. Use them to open doors, but once you're through them, take over.

- Keep in touch with your contacts. Don't let your network die from neglect.

5

APPLYING YOUR NETWORKING SKILLS

So far we have been concentrating on bringing you up to speed in the four core skills that are the underpinnings to all effective networking. To recap these are:

- picking the right people to network with;
- putting yourself across to these people in the best possible light;
- controlling the messages you feed out to them;
- responding to the messages they feed to you.

Given that you constantly strive to perfect these skills, the two-way traffic on your networking superhighway will keep flowing. You will have a powerful force at your fingertips and all you will have to do is unleash it when you need it and stand by for the results.

GETTING YOUR CAREER BREAKS BY NETWORKING

If you're newly qualified or if you're seeking to make a change in your career, the power of networking can help you to get the breaks. How? The answer is in two ways.

The first is by using your network as a source of advice on career choices. For example, if you're toying with the idea of becoming a doctor, do you know anyone who is a doctor? Alternatively, do any of your contacts know anyone who is a doctor? You will find first-hand information straight from the horse's mouth very useful to you when faced with important decisions such as these.

The second is by networking your way into your first career job (because of your lack of experience, this could be one of the toughest hurdles you ever have to face). Here you need someone to effect an introduction for you, a contact who can put a word in the right ears – for example, someone who already works for the organization you wish to join. Where competition for jobs is intense – as it often is with career starts – using your network to effect an introduction is a way of making sure you stand out from the crowd. Put simply, if the string is there, make sure you pull it.

WARNING!

Back to ensuring you always pick the right people to network with. If your introduction is effected by someone who is held in high esteem by an employer, it will go a long way towards smoothing your path to getting the job. On the other hand, if the person who introduces you is viewed as ineffective or lazy, you will, by association, be tarred with the same brush.

Your success in your new job (and how long you last in it!) will depend to a large extent on the links you forge with your bosses and the people you work with. Your lifelong interview obviously has a big part to play in this (keeping your image squeaky clean), but, at the same time, always

---

TIP

Getting starts in life can be very tough, especially at the beginning of your career when your professional network is at its smallest and least able to help (consisting perhaps of just a handful of contacts from university or the jobs you did during your holidays). So how do you go about getting your foot in the door when you don't actually know anyone on the inside?

The answer is the 'Trojan Horse Technique' – the reason for the name will become apparent shortly.

Whilst career-start jobs may be very thin on the ground, especially in times of economic recession, what is always in relatively abundant supply is low-grade, low-skill work, much of it temporary and/or part time. The trick is to worm your way into organizations in one of these lowly capacities then attack them from the inside – rather like the Greeks did at the Battle of Troy. Your weapon, in this instance, will be the power of your networking. Your presence in an organization will enable you to forge links with people at all levels – something that would not be possible for you to do from the outside.

Note: There's a lot more about the Trojan Horse Technique and its application in our book *The Power of Networking* (Kogan Page, 1999). It can be used in any situation where getting your foot in the door is difficult.

---

have special regard for people who can influence outcomes for you or who you depend on for advice and guidance (people who could tip the scales for you as far as your success or failure is concerned). Remember the tip about those little acts of kindness (the case study of Dean and Florence on pages 18–20). Doing the fetching and carrying for someone or making a cup of coffee for them when they're busy can go a very long way.

USING YOUR NETWORKS TO ACCESS PROMOTION

This is where you need to focus on one of your more important professional relationships – the relationship between you and your boss. Your boss will figure largely in any decisions about your future, so your chances of promotion will be greatly enhanced by any favourable impressions you manage to make – which brings us back again to the life-long interview and the importance of projecting a person-perfect and work-perfect image every day. But to see how this works in practice – and to draw out a few further lessons – let's take a look at another case study. This time the tale is told by Charles, the chief executive of a large manufacturing company.

Charles: A few months ago I had the job of picking a successor for the Operations Director who retires in six months. What I needed for this position was a good team leader, someone who would inspire confidence in the workforce and, at the same, introduce some discipline. Out of all the talent available, why did I go for John? For the simple reason that I had the good fortune to work for him when I first joined the company as a graduate trainee 15 years ago (he was a section head at the time). What I liked most about John was the way he always led by example, setting high standards both for himself and for his subordinates, correcting where necessary and never forgetting to give praise where praise was due. It was John I had to thank for my first big break with the company. He put my name forward to manage the project when we brought our first completely computerized production line on stream. He was also there to offer any advice – and came to my rescue a few times when I rubbed the factory management team up the wrong way!

I think John will make an excellent operations director. It's a promotion he certainly deserves.

The points to pick out from this case study are as follows:

- John made an excellent job of his lifelong interview. He maximized any benefits from his long-standing relationship with the upwardly mobile Charles.
- Charles was once John's subordinate – illustrating how your lifelong interview always needs to have a 360 degree orientation to it.
- Evidence of having a good networking relationship with your boss is when he or she is actively looking after your best interests and ensuring that your ambitions are fulfilled.

YOUR NETWORK AS A SOURCE OF INFORMATION

We have touched on this briefly already. Your contacts can act as a source of information and this can work for you in two ways. In the first scenario, you need to know something (eg the low-down on a company you are thinking of joining), so you ring round your professional network to see if anyone can help. In the second, one of your contacts hears of something that would be beneficial for you to know, so they ring you.

> *Karen:* I found out that my company was up for sale from an outside contact who overheard a conversation in a hotel where she was staying. This enabled me to start getting some irons in the fire quickly and, as a result, I had two job offers in my hand when the announcement was made that we'd been taken over by the biggest bunch of sharks in the industry!

Information fed to you through your network is often information that would be difficult or impossible for you to access by any other means. To have a source like this at your fingertips is, therefore, one of the many bonuses you will get from improving your networking skills.

NETWORKING FOR JOBS

Does it surprise you to learn that 50 per cent of jobs are filled by networking and even higher figures have been quoted for top-drawer jobs? What this points to is the ever-increasing importance of the so-called 'invisible job market' – the jobs that are never advertised; the jobs that are hard to find out about; the jobs that are often the best jobs.

So how can you access jobs like these? How will your improved networking skills help you to penetrate the mysterious world of the invisible job market? Jobs can be sourced by both proactive and reactive networking. Here's how:

Proactive. Ringing round contacts who work for other employers to see if they know of anything suitable for you. If so, getting your contacts to effect the introductions. (This kind of activity has a habit of being sparked off by an event – such as being made redundant or getting a poor pay increase.)

Reactive. Receiving unsolicited approaches either direct from contacts or through intermediaries (including consultants).

How successful you are at sourcing jobs by proactive and reactive networking depends largely on how successful you have been at projecting the right image through the medium of your lifelong interview. For instance, if Jack asks Jill to help by finding him a job with her firm, Jill will want to feel pretty sure about him before she proceeds. Similarly, if Jill is asked by her principals to suggest someone who might be suitable for a job, she needs to feel very confident about Jack before putting his name forward.

GETTING HEADHUNTED

Headhunting has given reactive networking a further and very exciting dimension. Headhunters operate at the very top end of the job market, so an approach from one is a pretty sure sign you're on your way up (that's the exciting part).

How do headhunters work? The answer is that they thrive on their contacts in the business world – contacts they take great pains to cultivate. So, whenever one of their clients comes up with a recruitment need, the headhunters ring round their network of contacts to see if anyone can provide the names of suitable candidates (candidates the headhunters then approach). Where this works for you is where your networking skills have brought you into contact with someone who is on a headhunter's list of telephone numbers. This is how you end up getting those mysterious telephone calls from people you've never heard of before.

Important: Headhunters sell themselves by reputation, hence the very last thing any of them want is to place a candidate with a client who subsequently turns out to be a duffer. With future billings at stake they play safe (always). So don't expect to be headhunted for a top job until you have mastered your lifelong interview skills and managed to project a person-perfect and work-perfect image to those who you network with.

USING YOUR NETWORK TO SOURCE BUSINESS

Contacts are lifeblood as far as people in sales are concerned. Contacts form a major part of marketing their skills to prospective employers.

But, with the increasing number of people who work in one-man/one-woman businesses or other small enterprises, professional networking as a source of business has assumed a wider importance.

First, a fairly typical experience:

> *Stella:* I'm a graphic designer and I went freelance a couple of years ago because I saw it as a way of making more money. I put a mailshot round the trade advertising my services but found, much to my surprise, it yielded practically zilch. Where does my business come from today? The answer is the advertising agency where I used to work – plus a few clients who came to me by recommendation.

Like many others, Stella has discovered it's far easier to get work where your face is known. Lifelong interview in action again? Yes, you've got it right in one, but here's another piece of advice to bear in mind:

TIP

For people who're in business on their own account, an important source of work is often their previous employers. It is vital therefore always to leave jobs on good terms. So don't, whatever you do, see handing in your resignation as the opportunity to get a few long-standing grouses off your chest or harangue the boss with a list of home truths. Instead bite your tongue, complete any outstanding work to the very best of your ability and leave with your person-perfect and work-perfect image fully intact.

GOING INTO BUSINESS WITH PEOPLE YOU NETWORK WITH

For those concerned, choosing someone to go into business with is a very important decision. **Get it right** and you could go on to do great things together. **Get it wrong** and your business partnership could become the business partnership from hell.

Choosing a business partner from among the circle of people you network with professionally has many advantages:

- You'll be looking at people you know and, because you network with them, they will be people who have come up to standard as far as your selection test is concerned.

- The bond of common interest and shared experience ensures like-mindedness as far as matters of principle are concerned (absence of like-mindedness on matters of principle is a common reason for people in partnerships falling out).

- The bonding agent will also be there to enable you to transcend the bickering and minor disagreements that are a normal part of life in any small business enterprise. The business is ensured a life that goes on after the strife.

TIP

Short of actually going into business together, people in networking relationships often have the capacity to combine their talents for mutual profit. For example, if you are a builder and if you network with someone who is an architectural technician, you can team up together to offer one of your clients a complete design and build package. At the end you split the proceeds then go your separate ways – until the next need arises, that is.

ACTION NOTEPAD

- Make your network work for you. Don't be afraid to use it. The more traffic on it, the better it performs.
- Get your career breaks by networking. Find the back ways into organizations that are difficult to penetrate.
- When it comes to projecting a person-perfect and work-perfect image, don't forget your peers and subordinates. Remember, networks are for life and, in years to come, peers and subordinates could be in positions to influence important outcomes for you.
- Share information with your network contacts. Tell them if you hear anything that's potentially useful to them. Reap the benefit of having information passed back to you in return.

- Turn to your network in moments of need. If you're made redundant, for example, get your contacts to see what employment opportunities they can unearth for you. The same goes when your career is in a rut and going nowhere.

- Networking is your way into the elusive invisible job market. Take special note if you're aspiring to jobs at the top of the tree. Work on your person-perfect and work-perfect image to enhance your chances of receiving approaches from headhunters.

- If your livelihood depends on sourcing business, see your network as there to help you. As a general rule, people who network with you will be happy to give you work. Remember to do the same for them if the positions are ever reversed.

- If you work freelance or as part of a small enterprise, identify opportunities for teaming up with networking contacts and profiting from combined effort.

Do you want to learn more about professional networking?

Our book *The Power of Networking* is available from all leading bookshops or by visiting the Kogan Page Web site at www.kogan-page.co.uk. Alternatively, you can e-mail orders to: orders@kogan-page.co.uk.

6

DOS AND DON'TS OF EFFECTIVE NETWORKING

DO:

- network with people who can influence positive outcomes for you;
- put effort into projecting a person-perfect and work-perfect image at all times;
- have the time of day for your network contacts;
- advise your contacts if your phone number changes or you move jobs;
- check your messages and e-mails regularly and consistently;
- get back to people when you say you will;
- make sure your contacts know what you expect from them;

- use your networks;
- leave jobs on good terms.

DON'T:

- network with people you don't know;
- network with people who could let you down;
- try to network with people with whom you've got no common interest or shared experience;
- let people you work with in on your darker secrets (keep them to yourself);
- use your network for gossip and spreading rumours;
- lose touch with contacts;
- miss opportunities for using your networking skills.

30 Minutes
... To Market Yourself
Yourself

Tony Atherton

**KOGAN
PAGE**

YOURS TO HAVE AND TO HOLD

BUT NOT TO COPY

Kogan Page Limited
120 Pentonville Road
London N1 9JN

British Library Cataloguing in Publication Data
A CIP record for this book is available from the British Library.

ISBN 0 7494 2943 7

Typeset by The Florence Group, Stoodleigh, Devon

Printed and bound in Great Britain by Clays Ltd, St Ives Plc

CONTENTS

The 30 Minutes Series

The *Kogan Page 30 Minutes Series* has been devised to give your confidence a boost when faced with tackling a new skill or challenge for the first time.

So the next time you're thrown in at the deep end and want to bring your skills up to scratch or pep up your career prospects, turn to the *30 Minutes Series* for help!

Titles available are:

30 Minutes Before Your Job Interview

30 Minutes Before a Meeting

30 Minutes Before a Presentation

30 Minutes to Boost Your Communication Skills

30 Minutes to Brainstorm Great Ideas

30 Minutes to Deal with Difficult People

30 Minutes to Succeed in Business Writing

30 Minutes to Master the Internet

30 Minutes to Make the Right Decision

30 Minutes to Make the Right Impression

30 Minutes to Plan a Project

30 Minutes to Prepare a Job Application

30 Minutes to Write a Business Plan

30 Minutes to Write a Marketing Plan

30 Minutes to Write a Report

30 Minutes to Write Sales Letters

Available from all good booksellers.
For further information on the series, please contact:

Kogan Page, 120 Pentonville Road, London N1 9JN
Tel: 0171 278 0433 Fax: 0171 837 6348

1

WHY MARKET YOURSELF?

How do you answer the question, 'What do you do?'

Companies look very carefully at what employees contribute to the corporate good these days, more so than used to be the case. In the 'leaner and fitter' organizations of today, with privatization, fiercer markets and global competition, every employee has to be seen to add value to the organization.

Busy managers may not always remember or even notice work that you are particularly proud of. If they are to know that your contribution is a bit special then you have to find pleasant ways of telling them. After all it is your career, not theirs.

Marketing yourself, in a gentle and gracious way, will help you. Having a memorable answer to the question, 'What do you do?' is a good starting point. It is certainly very good practice for the day when you may want to impress someone outside your company, at a job interview perhaps.

What do you do?

Your answer probably depends on who is asking and what the circumstances are. To a stranger at a party you may give a fairly short and general answer before asking them the same question. To an inquisitive child you give another answer, to prospective parents-in-law still another. To your newly-appointed Chief Executive you would give quite a different answer, with some detail, while still keeping it short enough to prevent his or her eyes glazing over. Most people think up answers on the spot with very little time to think; as a result their words will not be as punchy or as memorable as they might have been.

Some people are prepared for questions like this, especially if they know the new Chief Executive is along the corridor and heading their way. They give memorable answers to such questions. Memorable answers raise your profile and they may produce an invitation to contribute to the more exciting things happening in your organization and so help to build your career.

Such moments can be the decision times in your career when you get to choose between continuing along your current pathway or setting off down a new one that leads onwards and upwards.

For every answer to 'What do you do?' that is interesting and exciting there are at least ten that are dull and uninspiring. What are your answers like?

A training manager might answer:

I'm the Training Manager. I look after people's training needs, arrange courses, chase people who are late, keep the records, and so on.

Or:

> Me? I help to keep us in business by ensuring that our people have the right knowledge, skills and attitudes in the right place at the right time so that our customers are delighted and come back for more. I'm the Training Manager.

Both answers are accurate in as far as they go, but we hardly need to ask which will be remembered.

Think about how you normally answer the simple question, 'What do you do?' Write down some good answers for different situations and people. Read them out aloud and practise saying them – but do not let it become like reciting a script.

Profile questions

There are many similar questions, sometimes called 'profile questions', and all are variations on a theme – you. Can you give memorable answers to these profile questions? Keep your answers to less than 75 words.

- What do you do?
- Tell me about your career.
- What have you done this week?
- How are things?
- Tell me about yourself.
- What is your proudest achievement?
- What do you have to offer (main strengths)?
- Why do you want a career move?

What is 'marketing yourself'?

Using words like 'marketing' and 'selling' may seem odd when applied to you and your career but they are perfectly valid terms to describe what can be done. Of course, the practicalities of marketing and selling yourself are different from those of marketing and selling petrol or washing powder, although the principles are much the same.

We all know talented and respected people who are passed over in the promotion stakes because they do not 'sell' themselves. We may think we know others who have 'done well' with little talent, who have more froth than substance. Would better self-marketing have helped the former? Did the latter progress with the help of good marketing of a poor product?

It is a truism that, whoever you are, the art of gently marketing and selling yourself (but not being arrogant and pushy) can help you to be more successful in your career – if that is what you want. In this book we look at how you can do this – graciously but successfully. But what does marketing and selling yourself actually mean?

Marketing can be defined as the process of identifying, anticipating and supplying customers' needs at a profit. Selling is the part where you persuade the customer to buy. They are inextricably linked.

You need to both market and sell yourself because your career is a product in a market. Your customer is your employer, especially your manager. Other managers and employers are potential customers. Your product is what you do – hence the stress on the earlier question, 'What do you do?' Marketing therefore involves:

■ Understanding your market and how it is changing, knowing what is wanted now and in the future. *What is happening out there?*

■ Understanding your current product and changing it to meet future needs, matching it to the market. *What do I have to offer and what will I need to offer in the future?*

8

- Pricing your product and getting it to the customers. *How much am I worth and where do I want to work?*
- Promoting your product by building customer awareness. *How do I tell and show others what I can do?*
- Selling your product. *How do I convince them?*

Should you market yourself?

You already do. You have already marketed yourself on numerous occasions: you just did not think of it in those terms. You marketed yourself when:

- You tried at school to convince someone to include you in their team.
- You applied for a job.
- You answered an interview question.
- You tried to look smart for a VIP visit.
- You did a job especially well.
- You gave a speech.

If your aim is to be more successful in your career, to achieve fulfilment by using your talents to the full, to climb the ladder of promotion and get more interesting work, then gently marketing and selling yourself is important. As with anything else you will get more benefit if you learn the skills and use them well. So learn the rules and imitate the best; and do it nicely without exaggeration or misrepresentation.

You – a product

In marketing terms you are a product or service and a very complex one at that. You have different aspects to your life and many different roles.

At work you are an employee, perhaps a specialist or professional. Maybe you are also an employer, a manager, supervisor, coach, mentor, leader, counsellor and lots of other things besides.

Outside work you may be a parent, a child, a spouse, an aunt or uncle, a nephew or niece, a friend, a neighbour. Maybe you have a hobby or are a member or an official in a club, society, or church. All of these, and many more, are roles you have in life – aspects of you the product.

Within each role you will have aspirations. To achieve them you need the help of others. At work someone has to pick you for the next exciting project, select you for promotion, delegate to you the next challenging task. How will they know you are interested and able if you do not tell them? Your aspirations may be crystal clear to you but they are as dense fog to others unless you tell them.

How people see you determines how they think of you, whether you spring to their mind when they are looking for someone and whether you are seen as the best choice, an acceptable choice, someone to avoid, or whether you are not thought of at all.

Whether their reaction to you is positive or negative may depend more on what they think of you than on your actual talent. Their image of you comes from you and from others. You cannot control that image but you can influence it.

Selectively volunteering for exciting tasks or projects is a good way to spread the word about you, but you cannot know of every opportunity in your company. The only way you can be considered for roles or posts you are unaware of is for the person in charge to think of you or be told about you. Market yourself and that might happen. Keep quiet and it will not.

Ethics

We have all seen advertising campaigns that are full of hype. Like a soap bubble they are bright and shiny but there is nothing inside. You may have that view of some people whose methods you question. Their methods may be effective for a while but they bring no credit to those involved.

In this book I assume you are good at your profession and want to be even better, using your talents to the full to the benefit of yourself and others. I also assume you want to make legitimate progress in your career while providing a good and professional service to your customer, your employer. You have a good product to promote and you want to do that legitimately and honourably. This is no bluffer's guide.

Your self-marketing mission is simply:

To bring yourself to the attention of others without hype, misrepresentation or false promise.

Be positive

How you describe yourself is very important and we have already seen how your answer to one simple question, 'What do you do?' can leave an image of you that may or may not be helpful.

Consider two contrasting replies to another simple question, 'How are things?' The first is a typical downbeat meaningless reply and you will have heard it, or something like it, hundreds of times. The second is a paraphrase of a reply made by a very successful young manager.

11

1 'Oh, ok. Muddling through. You know how it is.'

2 'Ever busier. Still expanding. Was in New York last week buying a company. Only a small one but it gets us in the market.'

Of course, you cannot often give a startling reply like the second but you can always avoid negative ones like the first. Successful companies praise their products. Learn from them while avoiding their hype.

Listen to people around you and see how often negative replies are given to the simple 'How are things?' type of question. Always try to give a positive answer: you are describing your product. Include just one or two short facts.

Of course, no one wants a 30-minute monologue in answer to a simple social question. Positive answers can be overdone and achieve the opposite of their intent. Strike the right note by being positive without boasting.

An extreme example of a negative reply was given by the head of a chain of jewellery shops when he was asked how he could produce such inexpensive silver-ware. His joke, 'Because it's crap,' led to the demise of his chain of shops and the loss of his name from the high street.

A housewife and mother of three was asked, 'Do you work?'

Actually, I do work. I'm involved in a programme of social development. At present I'm working with three age groups. First, toddlers: that involves a basic grasp of child psychology and medicine. Second, teenagers. I confess the programme is not going too well in that area. Third, in the evenings and at weekends I work with a man aged thirty-nine who is exhibiting all the classic symptoms of mid-life crisis – that's mainly psychiatric work. For the whole job you have to be a brilliant planner, have a 'can-do' mentality and have a degree in conflict resolution. I used to be an international fashion model, but I got bored.

(Rob Parsons, *The Sixty Minute Marriage*, Hodder & Stoughton, 1997)

2

ME PLC

It can be enlightening to think of yourself, for a moment, as a company: Me plc.

Companies usually have several divisions or departments that look after various aspects of the business. Typically there will be a production or service department, a research and development group, and departments for administration, marketing, selling and so on. Each of these has a parallel in your career.

Production

What does the production or service department in your company actually do? The people there usually produce the goods or deliver the service for existing contracts. They do this cost-effectively while always looking for ways to improve. As new products are introduced they manufacture them to their traditional high standards, so helping to secure the future while being firmly rooted in the present.

Your 'production' is to keep your present job going as effectively as possible while seeking to improve and respond to changes that occur. For many people this is the height of their ambition and they find it satisfying and fulfilling. Their greatest challenge may be responding to changes but essentially 'production' is about keeping the present role or job.

R&D

A research and development group (R&D) looks much further into the future. They develop the next generation of products. In Me plc this involves deciding what future role or job you want and learning and planning for it – a central aspect of marketing.

R&D means preparing yourself for the next step up the ladder. Can you be one of the first into a new development in your specialism? Should you prepare yourself for management? If you are a manager, can you plan your move into higher management? R&D is all about learning, acquiring new skills, and developing new behaviours and attitudes. Take a wider and longer-term view than you do now and support this with self-development, training and wider experience.

Administration

Administration is about keeping records, maintaining contact with people, and keeping abreast of necessary non-professional changes such as IT. None of it is very exciting and few people actually enjoy it. Do it, but keep it simple.

Records

Keep records of previous jobs and projects – just the main aspects, such as what you did, costs, profit levels and who else was involved. Such details make it much easier later on if you want to describe what you have done to someone, say in an interview.

Record your own training and the things you have learned from projects, jobs, books and so on. Professional institutions call this a professional development record (PDR). If you have not seen one, ask around for a sample.

Keep a list of contacts, simply the name and address, etc, plus brief notes of when, where and why you met.

CV

Keep a record of new achievements in your professional life and update it periodically. This will be very helpful when you next apply for a job in your present company or another one. Use it to update your CV every six months or so.

Marketing and selling

Marketing is about deciding where you fit in at the moment and finding out what the future might be like (market research) and planning the changes you want to make. It also involves 'advertising' – making people more aware of your talents. Selling is about making the changes. The distinction between the two can become blurred but it is what you do that matters, not what you call it.

Conclusion

Seeing yourself as a small company, Me plc, can offer some insights into how to move your career forward. The production people are vital to the success of any company but they do not usually provide the vision that makes it grow. It is tempting to concentrate on production because it is immediate, but if your career becomes 100 per cent production you will only grow by accident.

If you want your career to progress, put time into:

- Finding out what lies ahead (market research).
- Planning and learning for the future (R&D).
- Recording information about yourself and your contacts (admin).
- Marketing and selling yourself.

Action

> What specific action have you taken in the last year to improve your 'departments'?
>
> - Production
> - R&D
> - Administration
> - Marketing and Selling

If almost all your action has been in production then you are doing very little to market yourself – as yet.

MARKETING

The four Ps

Ask someone who works in marketing what their profession is about and they will tell you about the 'marketing mix' or strategy that consists of the 'four Ps':

- *Product:* Defining the product in terms of what it is, its appeal in the market place, who it is for, what the next generation will be like, how to differentiate it from its competitors, and so on.
- *Price:* Deciding the price or prices.
- *Place:* Deciding how and where to distribute and sell it.
- *Promotion:* Bringing its existence to the attention of buyers by promoting it through advertising and other means.

All four aspects of this 'marketing mix' are important in helping you to market yourself, especially understanding your product (What do you do?) and planning your promotion (How do you tell them you do it?).

To illustrate these four Ps let's imagine we want to launch a new bar of chocolate. We will have to do very well indeed to succeed against established producers like Mars, Nestlé, Cadburys and the like.

- *Product:* Market research will help us to decide, with no guarantee of success, what people say they will buy. Is there room for another Mars type, Kit Kat type, Fruit and Nut type, or any other type? Will it be long and thin or short and fat, a square, a cube or a sphere? What distinctive flavour will it have? Will people break it into pieces like a Kit Kat or bite it like a Mars?

- *Price:* Checking in local shops reveals a wide price range for more or less standard-sized bars of confectionery. How much is charged for image and reputation? Will we undercut the market leader?

- *Place:* How will we get it to the customer? Will we sell direct to retailers or via wholesalers? Will it appear in supermarkets, convenience stores, high street shops, newsagents, petrol stations and vending machines?

- *Promotion:* What image do we want to create (the gentle feminine Milk Tray, the energy-giving Mars, the evening glamour of After Eights)? How will we advertise? Will we associate it with a famous person?

Your product

Thinking of yourself as a 'product' or 'service' can be illuminating. We have looked at the profile questions, 'What do you do?' and 'How are things?' and seen that being prepared for such questions can help you to produce more memorable answers.

In a manner opposite to death by a thousand cuts, small things such as these can help to build your career by a sort of 'climb by a thousand steps'. Of course, we hope there will also be some career jumps along the way – an escalator or two.

> Build your career as a climb by a thousand steps, but keep your eyes open for any escalators going your way.

You will expect the profile questions at job interviews but variations can occur unexpectedly in other circumstances and, of course, they can be phrased in a hundred ways. Confident answers help that climb by a thousand steps. They portray a professional image of someone who knows what they are about and can describe it clearly and succinctly.

Most answers you give will fall on stony ground – life is like that – but a few will sow seeds and some of those seeds will germinate and grow. These will bring you into someone's thoughts when they want a good person for a special job – perhaps a move to a new, dynamic and growing department, an escalator going your way.

> A toilet cleaner at NASA was asked, 'What do you do?' He is said to have replied, 'I'm helping to put a man on the moon.'

Product life cycles

Every product ever invented has a life cycle. Products are invented and introduced to the market, they grow in sales, reach maturity, sales saturate and then go into decline and finally the product becomes extinct. Unfortunately, so it is with careers.

Some product life cycles are very short, some very long. Some toys are here today and gone tomorrow, whereas the electric light bulb has been with us for over 100 years. What phase of their life cycle would you say credit cards and cheque books are in?

Phases of the product life cycle:

- introduction;
- growth;
- maturity;
- saturation;
- decline;
- extinction.

How does this concept of life cycles affect you and your career?

Think of some products, industries and professions that are at different stages of their life cycles; some examples are shown in Table 3.1.

Your company, your industry and your profession all have life cycles which could be long, medium or short. They are all working their way from introduction to extinction.

What stage do you think each is at now? Tick the boxes in Table 3.2. Could any go into decline or reach extinction before you are ready to retire?

Is the risk high, medium or low that you will have to change your employer, industry, profession, or career?

Table 3.1. Examples of life cycles

	Industry	Profession	Politicians
Introduction	Bioelectronics	Geneticist	Newly-elected MP
Growth	DNA profiling	PC games writer	Junior cabinet post
Maturity	Electricity supply	Teaching	Senior cabinet post
Saturation	Ship building	Game warden	Elder statesman
Decline	Roof thatching	Bank clerk	Back benches
Extinction	Gas lighting	Stagecoach driver	Lost seat

Table 3.2. Life cycles for your profession, industry, employer and your career

	Your profession	Your industry	Your employer	Your career
Introduction				
Growth				
Maturity				
Saturation				
Decline				
Extinction				

New and improved

Some management gurus believe that many of us will have to change career at least once, perhaps twice, during our working lives. If the stage you have reached in your career life cycle is discouraging, the good news is that life cycles can often be extended. Companies try to extend the life cycle of a profitable product by reinventing it, introducing a 'new-and-improved' version. How many 'new-and-improved' domestic products have you bought?

Here are some examples of extended life cycles:

- Washing powders have the same name as decades ago but the formula has changed many times.

- Pedal cycles have been given a new lease of life as a result of health and fitness and environmental campaigns.

- Old pop songs are re-released or recorded by new singers.

The phases of your career can be extended. Periodically you will need a new-and-improved you, a Mk2 or 3 or 4. You will need to stretch your career, find a new escalator. But first, you need to thoroughly understand your market before you can 'design' this new-and-improved You, Mk2.

Conclusion

In marketing terms you are a product and you can promote yourself by practising answers to some profile questions. All products have a life cycle including your career, employer, industry and profession. Life cycles can sometimes be extended and sooner or later you will need to extend yours. Before planning how to extend it, you need to analyse your market and your current product.

4

ANALYSING YOUR MARKET

To successfully plan for your future, your Mk2, you need to understand the market you are in now and how it is changing. Two widely used tools for analysing markets might be of real use to you. They are the PEST analysis and Porter's five forces.

PEST analysis

This looks at how four external sets of factors might influence the market for a product, in this case your career. Because they are external, you have no influence over them but they can have a strong influence on you. What you can do is watch them, see how they change, try to understand them, and take appropriate action. These external factors are:

- political;
- economic;

- social; and

- technological.

In the case of careers it is worth treating everything as being 'external', including company and departmental issues. Often it is not just one factor in isolation that you need to watch, but the mix of effects from several.

Political factors

What political factors could affect your career, perhaps through your company or industry?

- International politics: regulations, trade agreements and clashes, GATT talks. European rules and directives have changed some industries, for instance fishing.

- National politics: privatizations produce both redundancies and opportunities. Deregulation can put new life into an industry, such as telecommunications. Government initiatives, starting or ending, can change a situation.

- Local politics: planning permission, green-belt areas, new roads. Company plans can fall foul of local regulations.

- Company politics, macro: opening or closure of divisions and factories, mergers and demergers, expansions and cutbacks, core business or diversification. Quality systems. Management fads.

- Company politics, micro: relationships with your boss can affect your career. Is your department stable? Could it be outsourced?

Try to foresee the effects that political movements and decisions are likely to have on your industry, profession, employer and career. What threats and opportunities do they raise? More than one person has made a career out of new initiatives such as ISO 9000 and Investors in People.

Economic factors

What economic factors could affect you? Think about:

- The national and international economies: are they heading for boom or bust and is your industry susceptible to them? (not all are).

- Is your company successful or struggling. Does it have sound financial backing?

- Is your department waxing or waning? Is the budget growing or being cut?

- Has your salary kept pace with the industry?

- How do your company's financial statements compare to those of your main competitors? Compare the Annual Reports.

Social factors

Is your profession or personal career susceptible to social patterns? There is a vast range of them, from divorce rates and one-parent families to out-of-town shopping centres, the rise of supermarket chains, the ageing population, sales of personal computers, the proliferation of mobile telephones, traffic jams, and so on.

Technological factors

Technology changes at an ever faster rate and we soon take new products for granted. Think of some products that were introduced or proliferated only a few years ago that are now taken for granted: call centres, CDs, laser printers, digital television, the tamagotchi, electronic organizers, e-mail, some cancer treatments, many medicines. All were brought about or strongly influenced by changes in technology.

Careers are changed by technology. A typist who will not learn word-processing is unemployable. Mobile phones have created a vast new industry. Technology changes some careers, creates new ones and destroys others. What is it doing to yours?

> What political, economic, social and technological factors could make an impact on your career, company, profession or industry?

Spend some quiet time thinking about these four factors and how they can create opportunities for you or pose threats to you. Brainstorm the issues, ideally with a friend. Then take time to think them through and feed your conclusions into your plans for your future.

Porter's five forces

This is another analytical tool used to study markets but with quite a different approach to that of the PEST. It is named after its originator, Michael Porter, and looks at the competitive structure of a market. You can use it to guide your thoughts on the competitive structure of the market for your career.

Michael Porter said there are five main forces that affect the competitiveness of a market. They are:

1 The threat of new people or companies entering the market.

2 The rivalry amongst existing competitors.

3 The bargaining power held by the buyers.

4 The bargaining power held by the sellers.

5 The threat of new substitute products or services.

New entry

Some professions and industries are easier to enter than others. Doctors are well protected, for example, and even have a medical register of who is allowed to practise. Others have less protection or none at all. How easy is it for someone to break into or take over your career?

Are you vulnerable to a threat from others:

- Experienced personnel made redundant elsewhere?

- Newly-qualified college leavers?

- Short-term contractors?

- Part-timers?

- Outsourcing – sub-contracting your department to another company?

- Less expensive staff from poorer countries?

Careers have been attacked and sunk by all of these 'new entries'. How can you repel boarders?

Rivalry

Some industries are cut throat, some are cosy. How much rivalry will there be from your colleagues for your next promotion? How many applicants will come from outside? Is there a policy to promote internally or from outside? Might that policy change? Will others accept different locations, hours, conditions and pay that you will not? How can you counter this?

Bargaining power of employers (buyers)

This increases when there is a surplus of skills in the market place, and drops when there is a shortage. How many good applicants were there when a similar job to yours was last advertised? Ask a friendly personnel officer or apply to an advertised job in another company to find out.

Bargaining power of employees (sellers)

The converse. Your power increases if there is a shortage of people with the required skills and decreases when there is a surplus. Think about how you choose where to buy milk during the day, and where you buy it late at night, when only a convenience store is open. Are you represented by a trade union or do you represent yourself? Which is best in your case?

Substitutes

Substitutes are products or services that could replace yours. They can be complete replacements, such as cars replacing horses or electronic calculators replacing slide rules, or they can be substitute distribution channels such as supermarkets selling petrol and filling stations selling groceries, and both replacing the milkman.

Is there a potential substitute for your career? We have all heard of people who have had to retrain to do other jobs, so it does happen. There are fewer bank clerks today because cash machines and supermarket check-outs have substituted for them. In some companies entire departments have been 'outsourced'. Could it happen to you?

Conclusion

Use the PEST analysis and Porter's five forces to think about your own position, your company's prosperity in its market and you in your market.

See yourself as a seller, supplying a buyer in competition with others, in a market where there could be potential new entrants or threatening substitutes. Identify the main issues. Summarize them in simple terms as opportunities and threats.

> **What is happening in your market?**

5

ANALYSING YOUR PRODUCT

When analysing your product you need:

- details of what it is now, but in more depth than you have had before – your achievements and skills;
- a definition of what you want it to become in response to the changing market, as learned from the PEST and Porter's analyses – your Mk2;
- a plan of how you will move from one to the other – your development plan.

Your achievements

When you need to answer a 'What do you do?' type question in depth it is better to give a 'What I have done' answer. Used to support a description of your product it provides the proof that your product actually works.

ople try to impress potential customers with
ions or tales of success. You can briefly recount
ur previous successes or achievements to people
as needed. This is a case of not hiding your light under a
bushel; more than that, in fact – it involves picking the best
light to shine to fit the circumstances.

Think back over the last three to five years (beyond that
it gets less and less relevant) and make a list of your main
achievements, not just the ones you feel particularly proud
of, but all of your main ones. Think of what you did, how
well you did it, the cost or profit, if relevant, and the time
taken, if relevant. Include numbers wherever possible and
check them for accuracy.

Later, you can select from these achievements to build
better profile statements and even target them at specific
people and circumstances by choosing achievements carefully.

When asked, 'What do you do?' expand your answer by
describing an achievement that is relevant and easily understood by the person asking the question. This is one reason
why keeping good records (Me plc admin; see Chapter 2)
is important and why you should update those records with
details of recent achievements.

Here are some examples:

- I have coached four of my staff to use the computer
  system, focusing on what we actually need and saving
  £600 in consultancy fees.
- I have made a half-hour presentation to the Board for
  a £100,000 business proposal which was accepted.
- I increased sales in the last quarter by 3 per cent.
- I persuaded Supplier X to give us a 10 per cent discount
  for the next two years.
- I worked all weekend on the emergency at Customer Y,
  and solved it for Monday morning.

> List your achievements. Fill several sheets of paper. *This is very difficult, but persevere. Once they start to flow you will get a long list.*

Your skills

You have certain professional skills. Outside your profession these are rare but inside it they are common and do not differentiate you from your competition. Even so, it is useful to ensure that people know about them.

However, some of your professional skills will be unusual. Make a list of these. Your achievements will help you to identify them and provide verification, when you need it, that you really do possess and use them.

> Make a list of your common and unusual professional skills.

Soft skills

You will not enter, let alone progress, in a profession without the basic professional skills, and progression will normally be limited without some of the more unusual skills. Your progression will also be seriously limited unless you possess what are often called 'soft skills', especially the interpersonal skills that relate to dealing with other people.

Use evidence of these soft skills in your answers to profile questions, and examples of when you have used them. In many circumstances these soft skills can be as important as, if not more important than, some of the professional ones. Here are some examples.

onal skills	_Interpersonal skills_
Creativity	Leadership
Dedication	Empathy
Integrity	Communication
Flexibility	Listening
Copes with pressure	Questioning
Good judgement	Probing
Good intuition	Getting on with people
Uses initiative	Putting people at ease
Self-motivated	Team worker
Positive attitude	Willing to help others
Logical thought	Communicates effectively
Goal oriented	Develops other people
Proactive	Shares credit
Flexible	Motivates others
Makes good decisions	Inspires others

Classifying skills

It may be helpful to try to classify all the skills you have identified into groups to see if there is a balance. A well-known system, suggested by Richard Bolles, is to use four headings under which to list your skills relating to:

- data;
- ideas;
- things;
- people.

Do the relative size of your groupings suggest some strengths and weaknesses or some areas for improvement?

SWOT analysis

Whether analysing your current situation or planning your future one very useful analytical tool is the SWOT analysis. It might be the most useful analysis you do.

SWOT stands for:

- Your *Strengths.*

- Your *Weaknesses.*

- The *Opportunities* offered in the market.

- The *Threats* posed in the market.

You have two types of strengths and weaknesses:

- *Visible* – the ones other people are aware of.

- *Hidden* – the ones other people are not aware of.

SWOT works best when applied to a specific issue rather than in a global, unfocused manner. To do this focus on specific issues you are facing and SWOT them one by one. Take larger or more global issues and break them down into parts and SWOT the parts. Here are some examples of subjects to SWOT:

- How well do I match my current market?

- Should I apply for the new opening in Department X?

- I need to be noticed more by the decision makers.

- It looks like we will be bought by/will buy Company X; what should I do?

- There is to be a new project team; should I apply?

- I have a new boss; what should I do?

- There is a major reorganization coming; how should I react?

Table 5.1. Example of SWOT analysis: my company has just been taken over

Strengths	Weaknesses
I am well thought of in this department	All my experience is with this one company
I am working on a long-term project	I know very little about the new company
That project is profitable	I have never led a full project
I am adaptable and flexible (hidden strength)	I struggle with the financial side (hidden weakness)
I have a new project management certificate	

Opportunities	Threats
New merged company is bigger	There will be some redundancies
We are expanding abroad	They are already strong in my area
Our new owner specializes in projects	The customer for my current work does not like the take-over
There will be new work groups formed	If they move our offices to theirs, it is 50 miles away and I hate commuting
There is a shortage of my skills outside	

Use the SWOT analysis as a general-purpose tool to attack any problem.

■ *Strengths.* What are your strengths relevant to this problem? Are they known to others? How can you reveal your hidden strengths?

- *Weaknesses.* What are your weaknesses relevant to this problem? Are they known to others? How can you improve them?
- *Opportunities.* What opportunities are there? What were identified through the PEST and Porter's analyses?
- *Threats.* What threats are there? What were identified from PEST and Porter?

The SWOT plan

Once you have completed a SWOT analysis use it to develop a plan to:

- match the opportunities to your strengths;
- make hidden strengths visible;
- minimize the threats or turn them into opportunities;
- improve visible weaknesses, turn them into strengths;
- improve your hidden weaknesses.

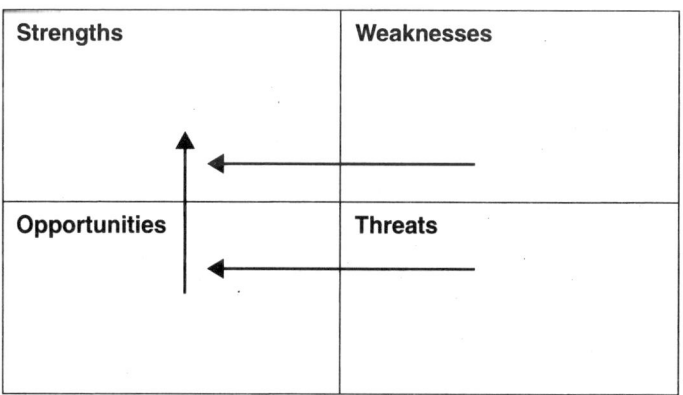

Figure 5.1. Turn weaknesses and threats into strengths and opportunities

Use SWOT analyses liberally and quickly. The more you use them the better you will become and the more useful they will be.

Definition of You Mk2

Now that you have learned more about yourself as a product and the market you are in, you are better able to define what you want to be in the future, say in three to five years time. Try to define what you will be in terms of:

- professional or specialist competence;
- managerial competence;
- position in the hierarchy;
- salary level.

Make your definition as specific as you can and give it a deadline. Consider alternative scenarios.

Development plan

Now you can seriously plan for your personal development (Me plc R&D; see Chapter 2). Look not just to strengthen current weaknesses but to build strengths for your future career position, your Mk2. Ensure that you have specific targets and the means of judging if they have been achieved, together with deadlines for when to achieve them.

The competition's SWOT

SWOT analyses can also be used to analyse your main competitors. Do the SWOT just as you would for yourself, although of course you will know less detail about them. Then plan what you have to do to compete with them.

6

PRICE

In comparison with defining your product, pricing your career is relatively straightforward. It involves not merely your salary, though that is likely to be the most important aspect, but also any perks you can reasonably expect to go with the job.

You are a cost

The cost to a company of employing you is greater than the cost of your salary because there are a number of overheads. Very roughly, you can say that it costs a company £10 an hour to employ you for every £10,000 of your annual salary. This allows for holidays and weekends, a 37-hour week, and a significant contribution to overheads.

Adding value

You can add value to a company either by bringing money in or preventing it from going out, ie by helping them to earn more or spend less. For the company to make a profit from you, on average you need to earn or save for them more than £10 for every £10,000 of your salary, every hour. If you exceed that figure then you are a financial contributor to the company, if not then you are a financial drain.

Knowing how much value you add to the company can be a very helpful statistic. It certainly gives a flavour to your achievements and demonstrates your eye for business, and adds zest to your answer to, 'What do you do?'

> Two accountants were asked what they do for the business. One said, 'I look after the books, check the figures, keep the finances ticking over.' The other replied, 'The most important thing I do is to make absolutely certain we get the cash flow right. Get that wrong and we're bankrupt no matter how full the order book is.' Which reply gets remembered?

Your price

Pricing policies can be very complex and determining salaries is no different. The company must make a profit out of you either by paying you less than you add or less than you save.

Personnel officers have access to guides and information that enable them to compare your salary to that of others inside and outside the company, but some jobs are hard to get comparisons for.

You can make your own comparisons, but be realistic. Here are some ideas:

- Swap details in confidence with people at similar levels in other departments or other companies.

- Consult salary surveys, especially those from professional institutions (read the fine print to see what is included).

- See equivalent government positions; their salary bands are published.

- Monitor job advertisements – those as close to your own as you can find.

- Try the internet for job advertisements and surveys.

- Check perks: pension (contributory or non-contributory), accident insurance, medical insurance, car or allowance, petrol allowance, financial loans, bonuses, profit sharing, share or stock scheme, leisure facilities, subsidized lunches, and so on. Ask about the cost of each perk as they are all part of the gross pay.

Once you have the true picture then you may start to plan your argument for a pay rise or a move. Without the true picture, the counter-argument will wipe you out.

Differential pricing

If you are self-employed you may find that you have to charge different prices to different customers. This is a common practice and is called differential pricing. For example, the cost of a railway ticket is different for pensioners, students and commuters, and changes with the time of day.

7

PLACE

The third P, place, refers to the distribution channels used to get your product to the customer. Thinking of your career, place can refer to a variety of aspects of where you work; things such as:

- geographical location: country and county, town or countryside;
- time and distance taken to travel to work each day;
- type of organization: commerce, industry, retail, charity, etc;
- size: small, medium, large, national, multinational;
- headquarters or branch office;
- ownership: private, public, stock market quoted.

You might think some of these are important to you, others not. How might they affect your career?

- A large company may offer training with formal qualifications.
- A large company may offer the chance to move around.

- A large company may offer large or prestigious projects.

- You may like the idea of working for a famous company.

- A small company may offer greater flexibility of work and provide rapid and wide experience.

- A small company may offer rapid promotion as they expand.

- Travelling a lot each day to and from work may prevent you from gaining extra qualifications at evening class.

- Commuting can be very expensive.

- In a small company you will get to know everyone.

- In a large company you may feel like just a cog in a machine.

- You may get shares in a private company.

There are many variations. What do you want?

8

PROMOTION

In marketing terms promotion is not about moving to a more senior job: it is the art of bringing your product to the attention of potential buyers, in effect – advertising. It is not actually selling, although it may include what many people would regard as 'selling themselves'.

Objectives

The objectives of promotion can be summed up as:

- to increase the customer's awareness of your product or service;
- to convince them of its importance to them;
- to remind them of how it is different from its rivals.

You will probably want to make senior managers more aware of you and the contribution you make and can make to the company (your potential), and to remind those with whom you have worked before. You will need to list the people you are targeting. Also try to raise the awareness of your work outside the company.

No matter how excellent you are some of your colleagues will be just as good, if not better, at some aspects of your work. Remind your target audience of your particular strengths and your specialist skills. Remind yourself by revisiting your SWOT analysis and your achievements.

Avoid criticizing your competition. Competing with your colleagues for a promotion is a temporary situation; you still have to cooperate with them the rest of the time. Good managers will always look for cooperative team players.

Avoid gross exaggeration. The 'buyer beware' saying should not apply to you. Your buyers should not need to be wary: they have entrusted you with their business. Remember your mission as suggested in Chapter 1:

> To bring yourself to the attention of others without hype, misrepresentation or false promise.

Before we look at the methods you can use to promote yourself it will be as well to know who you are aiming at.

Target audience

There are two broad types of target audience: those you reach with a scatter-gun and those you reach with a sniper rifle.

Television advertising is a scatter-gun approach. It reaches a large number of unknown people even though aimed at specific groups such as children or adults. Your scatter-gun could include writing articles for specific magazines or journals and giving a presentation at a conference.

Direct mail is an example of the sniper approach. It is targeted at known people and often addressed by name. Sniper fire for you might be to go to meetings attended by specific people you want to reach, or to write a report for the Board or senior managers.

Sniper fire

Sniper fire is likely to be the most useful approach for you. Your ideas of where you want to get to, the You Mk2, should help you to think of the people who may be able to help you along the way. Without that work, targeting your promotional audience is going to be less effective than it could be.

Of course serendipity and chance play a part. But those who are well prepared are more likely to make good use of opportunities presented by chance than those who are not. This is what people mean when they talk about 'creating their own luck'.

Inside and outside your company, who are the people who could help to foster your career? Who can open opportunities to you and encourage you to use your abilities to the maximum? You need a stage on which to operate. Who controls access to the stage? Who selects the cast? Who can:

- Pick you for . . . a new team?
- Suggest your name for . . . a new project?
- Support your inclusion in . . . a committee?
- Tell you about . . . special tasks?
- Who can coach you in some special skill?

Motives

Again, a word about ethics. What is your motive for looking for help like this? Is it to become a contributing member of a higher team so that you can use your talents more fully? Or is it to claw your way over others? We all 'use' people to some degree but to what extent do we repay that use? Are you as willing to help as to be helped? If you are engaged in a two-way process of mutual help, even if your help is directed at a third party, then you are likely to have little to worry about from an ethical viewpoint.

Your sniper's list

So who is on your sniper's list? Think of people inside and outside your organization. Take any legitimate opportunity to meet the Chairman, the Chief Executive and any Director or head of division, including Personnel. If you are naturally reticent, practise your profile statements and try to be a little bolder, but do not become Attila the Hun.

Consider people you know in:

- your department: colleagues, subordinates, manager, manager's manager;
- neighbouring departments;
- other groups, sections, branches, sites;
- your professional life: acquaintances at meetings, committees;
- your suppliers and customers: the representatives you meet.

If appropriate, consider your family, friends, neighbours and other acquaintances.

Remember your colleagues and those in other work groups who can tell you what is going on, those who make up the grapevine. Often the grapevine will provide accurate information before the formal chains of communication grind into action.

Once you have your target list you can decide how to communicate, and what methods to use to promote yourself. Update the list from time to time.

When you approach people avoid asking for a favour. Usually it is better to ask for information or advice than for action. If they want to take action, let them volunteer. With your manager, you do the volunteering.

Scatter-gun approach

Your scatter-gun targets will be less well defined. Your objective is to reach people you have never met, mainly outside the company but not exclusively, people outside your circle. Your aim is to get your name known in your profession or industry.

There are various ways to do this. For example, you could make a presentation at a conference or simply attend a conference and meet people during the coffee and lunch breaks – this is a very common and successful way of meeting new people from within your profession. You can put your name in front of even more people, but without meeting them, by writing an article or even a letter for a specialist magazine.

Your scatter-gun targets are not specific people but groups of specific people at the places where they meet or correspond. Make a list of your possible scatter-gun targets such as:

- specialists and other professionals;
- people in other parts of your company;
- senior managers.

And where you can reach them:

- specialist magazines or journals;

- your company magazine;
- professional institute committees or meetings;
- other meetings;
- conferences: organizing, addressing or attending;
- action groups;
- as a company representative to . . .

Promotional methods

You are likely to use four types of promotional methods: the spoken word, your actions, your appearance, and the written word. You also need to be aware of your 'branding' and how you can influence it.

The spoken word

Your spoken words are one of the prime means of promoting yourself to other people. There are three main ways in which your spoken words are noticed: the times when you use your profile statements, the occasions when you make a presentation, and every time you speak and portray either a positive or negative image of yourself.

Profile statements

The profile statements we looked at earlier are important. They all derive from the 'Who are you?', 'What do you do?' and 'How are you?' base questions. Make your answers as pleasant, interesting and memorable as possible and not too long.

If you have already written some first attempts revisit them now and try to improve them. Can you include an achievement or two, with a couple of memorable facts – the proof of the pudding? Practise saying them out loud. Do they sound pompous or self-centred? Update and improve them periodically.

Presentations

Take any opportunity to make a presentation, provided of course that you know what to talk about and will not make a fool of yourself. There are three reasons why people shy away from making presentations:

1 They do not know the subject matter, or a colleague knows it better.

2 They lack presentation skills.

3 They are fearful of standing up and addressing a body of people.

All three are valid reasons but ideally you should only miss an opportunity because of the first. The other two can be addressed by attending training courses or reading books on presentation skills.

> Should it be part of your development plan to either read books on presentation skills or attend a training course?

There are two secrets to making a good presentation. Together they improve your performance and reduce, but do not eliminate, the butterflies. They are:

1 Thorough preparation.

2 Careful practice.

No matter how experienced you are at making presentations you should still practise beforehand when a new or particularly important presentation is to be made.

Making a presentation gives you a wonderful chance to make an impression on people, hopefully a good one. Inside your company you could be addressing senior managers or the Board. At an external meeting you could be addressing other professionals. All will give you 100 per cent attention for the next few minutes. A born sales person would eat their heart out for an opportunity like that. Do not miss it even if you are nervous. Often you will get opportunities for one-to-one conversations afterwards; use those as well.

Opportunities to prepare and make presentations are relatively common. If you really want to you should be able to make several a year, and each one puts you in the lime-light, so they do need to be good.

Look to see what external opportunities there are, such as at conferences, professional meetings (national or local), sales presentations, and so on. Improve your skills with in-company presentations first. Helping on internal training courses is one way of getting some practice.

Every time you speak

One manager I used to know was very competent at his job but whenever I met him I could guarantee he would give me every negative slant to the latest company change or initiative. Even when saying something positive his body language and tone of voice would be negative. Do you know people like that? What impression do they make on you? Might anyone be thinking of you like that?

Whether you try to or not you create an impression whenever you meet and talk with anyone else. That impression has two aspects: professional competence and personality. Their view of you rests not just on what you say but on how you say it. Every conversation contributes to whether someone sees you as:

- professionally competent or incompetent, and
- personally positive or negative.

Next time you are listening to someone on television, perhaps a politician, or a chat-show guest, or a news reporter, take note of how their behaviour influences you as much as their words. Notice their posture and stance, their facial expressions, their demeanour, the intonation of their voice and their choice of words.

Why not try to cultivate a positive and cheerful manner to go with your professional competence? Imitate the best.

Actions

The best advertising is a personal recommendation. So first and foremost you must perform *a good, professional job,* keeping up-to-date as necessary. That will help your Me plc Production department to keep going. Remember that you do not need to be the best to be successful; by definition not everyone can be the best. But life gets easier when you are noticeably better than average.

An engineer was made redundant after 20 years with the same company. His prospects looked bleak but he sent speculative applications to people he had met through his work. 'We thought about poaching you last year,' said one as they offered him a job, 'but we didn't want to upset your employer because they're our best customer.' The moral: the good impression you create by doing a good job may one day come back to serve you.

Second, stretch and *expand your professional skills.* Keep pace with the present (Me plc Production) and build for the future (Me plc R&D and You Mk2). Your personal development plan should include:

- training to learn new knowledge and skills or improve existing ones;

- coaching from those who can do things you want to learn, and coaching others;

- teaching yourself from books, CD-ROMs, videos and learning packages;

- learning from experience by volunteering for new tasks and projects.

Third, *develop your soft skills;* those personal and inter-personal skills that we highlighted earlier. When recruiting new staff it can be relatively easy to find people with the specialist knowledge and skills. Often it is much harder to find someone who can handle people and get the best from them. People skills can be the hardest to find so develop yours to the full.

Fourth, *look out for escalators.* If you have been involved in one challenging project you will want another one. Get into the newer and expanding areas of your company and get out of the older, shrinking areas. All companies have both; it's up to you to choose. Again, volunteering is the way. If you are given a task that is an old cabbage this time, complete it with a smile while trying to get a promise of a peach next time.

Fifth, to use a horrible word – *network.* In plain language, keep in touch with people, especially those who may be able to help you through advice and information – your sniper targets. And be sure to help them and others whenever you can, not so that they 'owe you a favour' – a very selfish attitude – but because that is what you are here for. In any case, being known as a helpful person is a desirable image.

Sixth, *associate with others.* At work it is natural to lunch with your immediate colleagues. Branch out and lunch with people from other departments and work groups. Listen to what is going on outside your group.

Finally, *be associated with success* – not as a hanger-on but as a contributor. To use that old saying, don't be a passenger be part of the crew – preferably the captain or navigator.

Appearance

Always try to look the part or slightly above it. In other words dress to suit the image of the successful person doing your job, or slightly better.

Knowing what this image is can sometimes be difficult. If you were going to an interview for a new job you would automatically dress to suit your image of the new position. Take note of how those senior to you dress and decide if you would like to imitate them. As in other areas, imitate the best if you are going to imitate anyone.

> In Hong Kong in the 1980s, then a British colony, some Chinese bankers dressed in pin-striped suits, wore bowler hats and carried rolled umbrellas. It looked like the City of London except that the humidity was in the 90s and the temperature was in the 30s (90s Fahrenheit).

> A well-established, dynamic British firm was bought by a youthful American firm. The American code of 'dress down' (jeans and tee shirts) flew in the face of the previous 'professional' look and almost caused hysteria. How many careers were damaged, unintentionally, by the feeling that they were 'not one of us'?

The written word

Every article, report, letter, memo and e-mail you write says something about you. They speak of your professional and technical competence and they portray an image that depends on your skill at writing. This image is portrayed both inside and outside the company.

Not everyone is naturally blessed with good writing skills. If you are not then try to approach your writing in three stages:

1 *Preparation.* Increase the time you spend preparing your material before starting to write. Gather your material together, organize it and sequence it first.

2 *Writing.* Write without stopping to make corrections (except for minor mistakes). This is a creative time so do not stop to criticize your work.

3 *Editing.* Now criticize it. Look for ways to use simpler words and shorter paragraphs. Check grammar and spelling and get someone who is good at grammar to check it for you. Good secretaries are ideal.

Books

Writing a successful professional book will get your name noticed, but it is a difficult feat to achieve. Most submissions to publishers are rejected. Note that:

- it needs a huge investment of your time, with no guarantee of success;

- you should write a letter to the publisher first; send a synopsis, a list of chapters and a sample chapter;

- check in bookshops for which publishers are publishing your type of work;

- tell your employer: they might help with facts and illustrations;

- you must not give away the business's secrets.

Articles

Target the magazines and journals that publish the type of articles you can write and are read by the people you want to reach inside and outside your company.

- Check the typical length and complexity.
- Check the style including sentence lengths, complexity of the words and jargon.
- Check their use of illustrations and photographs.
- Send a proposal rather than a manuscript and ask if they have guidelines for authors.
- Tell your employer and get any help they will give.

Reports

Reports may be internal or external. Many people dislike writing reports and your boss may welcome a volunteer. Make sure you are professionally happy with the content and try to ensure that your name goes on the cover along with his or hers. Write brief reports on your own work whenever you can. Sometimes reports are delivered with a verbal presentation. That may open an opportunity for you to make the presentation and join in the subsequent discussion.

Letters, memos, faxes and e-mail

Treat each one in a professional manner.

- Letters will usually be on good quality paper with a company letterhead and logo, both of which look professional and add authority.
- Memos are for internal use and may be less formal than a letter. Make yours slightly more formal than average so that they are more noticeable.

- Faxes and e-mail may be printed on cheap paper by the recipient. They may not have a company header or logo and so you have only your words to display your professionalism.

CV

Your CV is an advertising leaflet and exists only to promote you. Use your CV more widely than is traditional. Use it to promote yourself internally when you try to join another team or group as well as when applying for jobs outside the company.

- Include some of your achievements as proof of your ability; do not just list responsibilities.

- Focus on the last five or six years with only an outline of previous experience to show career development and continuity of work.

- Keep your standard CV up to date.

- Use no more than two pages of A4 white paper.

- When applying for a job rewrite your standard CV, focusing it on the particular job.

Branding

Branding is used to give a product an identity, to make it different from its competitors and secure customer loyalty. It is very powerful. For example some supermarket customers will ignore 'own brand' products, even when reduced to silly prices, in order to buy the traditional brand they have come to trust. The same can be true at work when managers are selecting a team for a prestigious new project and choose their old favourite people.

You already have a 'brand' whether you want one or not because branding exists in other people's views of you. You need to be aware of how people have branded you or 'see you' and, if necessary, influence them to re-brand you in a different way.

Branding can be a serious career problem after a company merger or a change of job. 'Old' staff quickly form impressions of what 'new' people are like: they are branded. There is a feeling of 'us and them' which lingers for a long time because of the different original cultures.

As two organizations merge occasions inevitably arise when managers have to select staff for a new project or post. When they favour staff from their old company, even if trying not to, that is branding. You may say they are simply choosing those they know best or know they can trust. Fine, but that is branding.

Here are some examples of people who are easily branded:

- students, young people, the over-50s;

- ex-forces personnel and ex-civil servants;

- headquarters staff;

- field staff.

Genuine quotations that reflect branding:

- About Research and Development staff: *'They're different in R&D.'*

- About the company accountants: *'They live on a different planet.'*

- About staff from the other company after a merger: *'They're a funny lot.'*

You are already branded to some degree. People already feel some sort of loyalty to you or not, they already feel some trust in you or not, they already feel some preference towards you or not. You can affect this image, this branding, in the ways described above by consciously trying to shift the image from a clone of Company A or B to a personal image or brand of you: Me plc.

Use the things you say and do to disassociate yourself from any negative images attached to your division, your group, even your profession (while retaining personal friendships and loyalties) and associate yourself with positive images by demonstrating your individuality and originality.

The best positive brand you can have is success, which brings us back to the general advice to: *Imitate the Best.*

Conclusion

Promotion is about increasing peoples' awareness of you so that they are more likely to 'choose' you. Use both sniper and scatter-gun approaches to reach your selected targets using the spoken word, the written word, your appearance and your actions. Identify and change any negative 'branding'.

SELLING

During or after every marketing campaign there comes a time when someone has to sell the product or service to a real customer. You too will face such occasions. These could be at a formal interview for a new job, or when meeting someone who is putting a new team or department together, or when meeting a senior manager whose group is expanding, or other similar situations. In all of these cases you will need to 'sell yourself'.

The six stages of selling

It is said that there are six stages in personal selling.

1 Gaining entry to the potential customer – the decision maker.
2 Identifying the needs of the customer.
3 Matching the features of your product or service to their needs.

4 Selling the benefits of your features by describing what the customer will experience.

5 Answering the inevitable objections that customers raise.

6 Closing the sale: moving them from intent to action.

These sales techniques are worth knowing about. Apart from being useful when defending yourself against a pushy sales person, they can be applied to furthering your career. Consider the most challenging example: a formal job interview.

Gaining entry

Your promotion efforts (the application letter, application form and CV) have gained an invitation. If it is an internal post you will have reminded the manager of achievements that he or she already knows about, plus some that are new to them.

Identify needs

The homework you did on the company and the job, coupled with carefully listening to what the interviewer tells you, should give you a picture of the customer's needs. When unsure of a point or two – ask. With an internal post quiz people you know in the department before the interview. What have been the successes and failures of this group? What new contracts and problems do they face? How will they approach them? Why has the new post been created?

Match features to needs

Mentally check how your knowledge, skills and attitudes/behaviours (such as dedication, motivation, etc) fit what is needed. Identify the key points in your mind.

Sell the benefits

Explain to the interviewer how your skills and experience provide what they are looking for. Relate to their problems by describing relevant achievements in your past and let them think about how similar successes could make life easier for them.

> Your situation here sounds similar to one in my last job. I devised a new system and implemented it. In the first year we reduced waste by 12 per cent, which was more than had been achieved in the previous three years.

Handle objections

Ask if there is anything they are not sure about. Are they satisfied that you have the necessary skills and experience and can do the job? Have they any reservations about offering you the job? (Can you really ask that? Yes!)

Close the sale

This is not always possible at a real interview – there may be other interviewees sat outside waiting their turn. Tell the interviewer that you still want the job, and why. Ask them when they will decide and when ideally they would like you to start. Let them know that you have other options but that this is your preference.

Selling the benefits is the most difficult stage apart from closing the sale. Look beyond the immediate problem to show how you can make life easier or better for them. You are professionally competent but so are all your competitors. How you sell yourself as a solution to their problems, and how well you will fit in with their team, are often the deciding factors.

> Analyse television advertisements to see how they sell to you. Any motor car will get you from A to B, any washing up liquid will clean your dishes, any bank will provide a credit card; so how do they try to persuade you that they are different from all the rest?

Sell the benefits you can bring, not just your skills. To paraphrase a once-famous television advertisement for sausages: sell the sizzle, not the sausage.

Referrals

Good sales people always ask for referrals, that is for the names of other people who might be interested in their product. Listen for the names of people who might be interested in you. Ask for 'referrals'. The best advertising is by word of mouth.

Conclusion

Learn the basics, the six stages of selling, and see how they can be applied to marketing you. Concentrate on 'selling the benefits, not the features' – the sizzle, not the sausage.

10

CONCLUSION

Personal satisfaction lies, at least in part, in using your talents to the full to achieve things for yourself and for others. Marketing yourself helps you to do that. It is nothing new. You have been doing it for years even if you didn't realize it.

Approached in the right spirit, gently and with integrity, it can help to build your future and fulfil your potential.

So, 'What do you do?'